Life
Reimagined

Richard J. LEIDER
Alan M. WEBBER

Life
Reimagined

Discovering Your New
Life Possibilities

BK Berrett–Koehler Publishers, Inc.
San Francisco, *www.bk–life.com*

LifeReimagined.org
Real Possibilities from **AARP**

Berrett-Koehler Publishers, Inc.
235 Montgomery Street, Suite 650
San Francisco, CA 94104-2916
Tel: (415) 288-0260   Fax: (415) 362-2512   www.bkconnection.com

Ordering Information

Quantity sales. Special discounts are available on quantity purchases by corporations, associations, and others. For details, contact the "Special Sales Department" at the Berrett-Koehler address above.

Individual sales. Berrett-Koehler publications are available through most bookstores. They can also be ordered directly from Berrett-Koehler: Tel: (800) 929-2929; Fax: (802) 864-7626; www.bkconnection.com

Orders for college textbook/course adoption use. Please contact Berrett-Koehler:
Tel: (800) 929-2929; Fax: (802) 864-7626.

Orders by U.S. trade bookstores and wholesalers. Please contact Ingram Publisher Services, Tel: (800) 509-4887; Fax: (800) 838-1149; E-mail: customer.service@ingrampublisherservices.com; or visit www. ingrampublisherservices.com/Ordering for details about electronic ordering.

Berrett-Koehler and the BK logo are registered trademarks of Berrett-Koehler Publishers, Inc. AARP is a nonprofit, nonpartisan organization, with a membership of more than 37 million, that helps people turn their goals and dreams into real possibilities, strengthens communities and fights for the issues that matter most to families such as healthcare, employment and income security, retirement planning, affordable utilities and protection from financial abuse.

Printed in the United States of America

Berrett-Koehler books are printed on long-lasting acid-free paper. When it is available, we choose paper that has been manufactured by environmentally responsible processes. These may include using trees grown in sustainable forests, incorporating recycled paper, minimizing chlorine in bleaching, or recycling the energy produced at the paper mill.

Library of Congress Cataloging-in-Publication Data
Leider, Richard.
Life reimagined : discovering your new life possibilities / Richard J. Leider and Alan M. Webber. — First edition.
    pages cm
  ISBN 978-1-60994-932-7 (pbk.)
1. Middle-aged persons—Psychology.   2. Middle-aged persons—Conduct of life.
3. Older people—Psychology.   4. Older people—Conduct of life.   5. Aging—
Psychological aspects.   I. Webber, Alan M., 1948–   II. Title.
HQ1059.4.L45 2013
305.244—dc23   2013026043

First Edition
18 17 16 15 14 13   10 9 8 7 6 5 4 3 2 1

Cover designer: Scott A. Davis
Book producer, text designer: Detta Penna
Copyeditor: John Bergez
Proofreader: Katherine Lee
Indexer: Kirsten Kite

Contents

Foreword

The authors of this book have given us a great gift. It is a gift of self-reliance, a gift of confidence, a gift of hope.

First and foremost, this book is personal. This book is about you. It is not a lecture—it's a conversation. Through the power of storytelling, Richard Leider and Alan Webber take you on a personal journey of fear and aspiration, risk and security, meaning and purpose. Their words and insights are inspiring and energizing. Their tools and techniques are realistic and practical. Their genius is not to help you reinvent your life, but to help you adapt and thrive in a new life phase.

This book is a road map for the "new normal" of reimagination and new choices that confronts so many people today in midlife and beyond. And you will discover that its message applies to younger adults who find themselves navigating major life transitions in a time of rapid change. Whatever your own phase in life, the road map shows you how to find the inspiration and courage to reimagine your direction, reassess your gifts, and unlock your personal potential. It will help you find "what's next" and discover your real possibilities as you move toward your best life regardless of age.

I am the Chief Brand Officer of AARP. I am also about to turn 50. I not only relate to the conversation in this book. I live it.

I am also first-generation American—a by-product of the Cuban revolution. By age 16, I was a caregiver to my father, who had cancer. I spent endless nights wondering how I was going to get through the experience and what the meaning of it all was. Shortly after his death, my mother was diagnosed with Alzheimer's. My caregiving for her did not end until her death.

By then, I was 28 years old. My parents never saw me graduate from college or get married; they never saw me become a U.S. Senate press secretary, CEO of a tech company, or senior partner of a global communications company. More important, they never met my son.

Through all those years, I lived a life of constant reimagination, and I instinctively went through all the steps you'll discover in this book. I formed my Sounding Board of friends and family to help me navigate, learn, grow, and achieve. In each transition I "repacked my bags" and started over—each time leaving something behind that was not useful for my next chapter. Learning to live in the present and taking one small step at a time was not a process in a book; it was my existence.

The life transitions kept coming. The economic collapse dealt me great financial stress at a time of profound personal challenge—a divorce, the death of my brother, and the role of single parenthood. I found myself a focus group of one, living and dealing with many of the same issues as the people I was hired to serve in my role as the chief steward of the AARP brand. The teacher became the student—and the student went to work.

Enter a Life Reimagined moment. One sleepless night, four years ago, I realized that my calling was to help millions of people navigate their personal "what's next" by developing smart solutions to life's challenges, a meaningful route to achievement, and the simplest way to understand the "new normal." And I had to do all of this while honoring the AARP promise of helping multiple generations live with dignity and purpose.

That's when I turned to Richard and Alan. They, along with others, went to work to activate a global network of thought leaders and to harvest the rich insights you will find in this book. I'm humbled by the commitment and intensity that Richard and Alan have brought to this enormous challenge. They have poured their lives' work into the pages that follow. As a result, we now have this modern road map and interactive guidance system for navigating a new life phase.

But as proud as I am of them, I'm even more moved by the commitment of A. Barry Rand, the CEO and "chief servant" of AARP. His leadership has prompted AARP to take an active role in this new conversation of "living versus aging" and to flex its mighty reach to bring the best thinkers, the latest resources, and the collective power of community to create the Life Reimagined platform. Our hope is that this platform will spark a movement that goes beyond a generation encountering aging to engage people of all ages in asking that fundamental set of questions, "What's next?" "What's next for *me?*" *"What's next for all of us?"*

So read this book as a gift to yourself. Play with the diagnostic tools. Chart your course toward your next possible life. Then pass it on to your spouse, your partner, your children, your friends—anyone you think will benefit from a new road map for the new normal. I wish I had had the insights in this book many years ago, when I was a 16-year-old caregiver trying to make sense of the chaos, the pain, or simply the aspiration of achieving my goals.

It's time for new personal solutions and new personal tools. It's time to reimagine your life's possibilities. Enjoy the journey!

Emilio Pardo
Executive Vice President
and Chief Brand Officer, AARP

Your Life Reimagined Journey

Let's start this book at the end.

In the end it's up to you.

Will you choose to take your Life Reimagined journey?
Will you choose to add your story to the thousands—the millions—of stories of curious, courageous pioneers of Life Reimagined?

Of course, it's up to you—to each of us—to make this choice.
But here's what's at stake. Here's why we genuinely believe you should choose to join us in taking the Life Reimagined journey.

The fact is, we are all participants in one of the most significant social movements of our time.

We are engaged in the creation of a new phase of life. We call it Life Reimagined.

This new life phase comes after middle age and before old age. Its impact—the idea of a Life Reimagined moment—can come at any age. This new phase of life renders obsolete the myths and conventional wisdom of the last 50 years, the old story that has defined the trajectory of our life course and constrained the choices available to us in the second half of life.

Life Reimagined says you can choose your own path at any step of your life journey. As we reimagine the way we live and age, we will reimagine every phase of life that comes before and after Life Reimagined. The consequences of each of us exercising choice in our lives will ripple across every generation and every phase of life. Very simply, we are living in a transformational time that is personal for each of us and universal for all of us.

What Is Life Reimagined?

Life Reimagined is three things.

First, it is a map and a guidance system to help people navigate a new phase of life.

Second, it is a growing community of people who, by the way they live their lives, demonstrate the power of possibilities in this new phase of life. They are Life Reimagined pioneers—they exemplify the map in action.

Third, it is an emerging social movement that cuts across all distinctions, including age. It is a movement that will change how we age—and in the process change how we live.

Why Life Reimagined?

Before you read any further, stop and look around you. Check the news. Listen—really listen—to what so many conversations today are all about. Pay attention to the underlying themes and emerging threads that define the times we live in.

If you pay close attention to the forces at work in the world today, you'll see why Life Reimagined makes sense—in fact, more than makes sense. Why it is necessary and inevitable, why it accurately and honestly captures the new reality of our lives.

First, we are living longer.

Since 1900, when life expectancy in the United States was 47 years, we've added more than three decades to the average life span. Those additional years change the whole trajectory of life—and what is possible for each of us to choose to do with those years.

Second, we are working longer and more productively.

Living longer means adding more income-producing years to our lives, whether by choice or by necessity. This new reality has far-reaching implications for generations to come. As you'll see, work and economics are a large component of Life Reimagined, though they are far from the whole story.

Third, we are living with meaning.

So much change in the world produces uncertainty—and uncertainty returns us to the fundamentals of what matters: our own purpose and our connections to others. Life Reimagined invites us to get in touch with the most authentic meanings in our lives—and to act on them to discover new possibilities and make new choices.

What Does Life Reimagined Say?

At the heart of Life Reimagined is a manifesto that calls upon each of us to live our lives with choice, curiosity, and courage.

It says that each of us is an experiment of one. That there are no one-size-fits-all answers for this new phase of life. Each of us has the freedom to choose our own way, in our own way, throughout all the years of our life. No old rules, no outdated social norms, no boundaries of convention or constraints of expectation.

It says that, in a world of change, there are two constants: having your own purpose and being connected to others.

It says that Life Reimagined is a journey of inner and outer discovery. And that the ultimate discovery each of us can make is self-discovery.

It says that none of us should go it alone on the journey into this new phase of life. Isolation is fatal.

Finally, it says that as we learn to reimagine this new phase of life, we will end up reimagining every phase of life. Thinking differently about how we live the second half of life will inevitably change how we live the years in the first half. As we understand the choices that are open to us as we age, we'll see that those choices are there for us at any time.

Strengthened by these truths, equipped with a map of the new territory that lies ahead, supported by the stories of countless pioneers of Life Reimagined whose real-life examples show the way forward, Life Reimagined offers each of us the promise of a life of real possibilities.

Mapping the Life Reimagined Territory

As pioneers of Life Reimagined, we are both exploring the territory and describing it as we go deeper into it. With each of our stories we add more detail and clarity to what lies ahead. Since everyone's life is an experiment of one, everyone's journey into the Life Reimagined territory will be unique.

That said, there is a map to make sense of this or any new phase of life. The map features six guideposts that can help you find your way on your individual journey. Don't think of these as steps to be taken in rigid, chronological order but as practices to guide your way:

Reflect: A call to pause before you start the journey and then at various steps along the way, understanding that change and choice occur from the inside out.

Connect: A step where you request feedback and counsel from trusted friends and guides, recognizing that isolation is fatal—no one should make this journey alone.

Explore: A beginning of the journey of discovery, a step of testing different possibilities, both inside and out, in the knowledge that curiosity and courage are essential to finding the way forward.

Choose: A narrowing of options in which you focus on your priorities and do both a deeper dive and a reality check, exploring a smaller number of choices to see which fit your emerging sense of what's right for you.

Repack: A step of deciding what's essential for the road ahead—what to let go of and what to keep, how to lighten your load, both tangible and intangible, for the new way that is opening up.

Act: A first step toward making the possibilities real in the recognition that taking action doesn't drain energy, it releases energy through the optimism that comes with choice, curiosity, and courage.

If you choose to follow this map wherever it leads you, you will be making the choice to become part of the community of Life Reimagined pioneers, whatever your age.

Here's the story of one person who made that choice.

A Game of Tag

Betty Smith hated her civil service job. A rail-thin woman into her twenties, after giving birth to her daughter she saw her weight balloon to more than 200 pounds. Her diet depended on junk food, and she had turned into a cigarette smoker.

This wasn't who she'd expected to be or how she'd expected to look in her thirties.

One day, Betty remembers, she found herself at the park with Tracy, her daughter, who wanted to play a game of tag.

"Mom," Tracy said, tagging her and running away, "you can't catch me!"

"The thing is," Betty says, "she was right. I was so out of shape and so out of breath. I decided I had to get off the path that I was on, or I wouldn't be around to see my daughter grow up."

That was a Life Reimagined moment for Betty.

It was a moment when she realized that she could make a

choice that would fundamentally change her life. It started with a change in her mindset, a change that altered how she saw her life going forward. Because of that moment, Betty saw with startling clarity a new purpose for her life and a new set of practices to help her achieve her life purpose. This Life Reimagined moment changed how she saw herself and how she experienced the world.

She quit smoking.

"I'd been casually saying, 'I shouldn't smoke,' as I was lighting up another one. But then I realized I needed to be there for my daughter," she says. "That was the passion that I had."

She worked out a meatless diet of fruits and vegetables, whole grains, beans, seeds, and nuts. When she traveled, even to places like France with its noted cuisine, she stuck to her diet, carrying cans of chickpeas to make sure she got enough protein.

She made the decision to begin a regimen of walking, and the pounds started to melt away. Walking gave way to running—first two miles a day, then four, then a 10K race. She entered marathons all over the world, and then took on ultramarathons. From ultramarathons she stepped it up even more, entering twenty-four– and forty-eight–hour races.

"I've been running for forty-three years, basically nonstop," Betty says, "and I've clocked well over 100,000 miles." In all, Betty has run more than seventy marathons, competing on every continent and in locations as exotic as the ice of Antarctica and the pyramids of Egypt.

That game of tag in the park also led her to look at her work life. She went back to school to get an undergraduate degree—and then added on an MA and a PhD. She jettisoned her boring civil service job and embarked on a thirty-year career in early childhood education.

"I've gotten to the point where I've been able to age agelessly," Betty says. "And I believe that each person can make a decision to age agelessly."

Now seventy-one, Betty says, "Everybody has got this inner strength inside. People don't realize they've got this strength and they don't pull on it. And the strength is just waiting there and it would love to be asked to be active."

Betty Smith's story is one story of Life Reimagined. It shows what is possible when you live with choice, curiosity, and courage. And it says that the opportunity for discovering new possibilities in life—possibilities that matter to us, on our own terms—is there at fifty, sixty, seventy—or thirty.

Who Is Life Reimagined For?

There are countless varieties of Life Reimagined stories. Some stories are about family and relationships, some about work and earning a living. Some are about achieving better health or mastering a new skill, some are about transcending tragedy or overcoming heartbreak. Some feature celebrities who have chosen how they will shape their lives, regardless of fame or fortune. Some tell the stories of ordinary people who choose to live by their own rules, seeking their own sense of fulfillment. The simple truth is, Life Reimagined touches all of us.

Life Reimagined is for people who may be pushed by pain or pulled by possibility.

It is for people who are driven by their fears or propelled by their aspirations. People who are ending a relationship, beginning a new one, or burnishing an existing one. People who are trying to make sense of their old way of life or seeking to explore a new one. People who are facing aging and retirement or looking to get started on their lives in uncertain economic times. People who are wrestling with money problems. Dealing with the demands of caregiving. Looking to establish a new identity that better reflects who they really are. People who are looking to find new meaning in a life grown dull.

In other words, it is for people who are in a Life Reimagined moment in their lives.

Living involves change. It's inevitable and desirable. To make good choices about change, we need guidance and direction, new life skills and new practices. Life Reimagined provides that guidance and those practices.

Here's the truth: the art of reimagining your life must be learned. The search for "what's next" in this new phase of life is driving one of the most powerful social movements of our time.

What's Next?

In the end the choice is yours.

In the end it's up to you.

Will you choose to take your Life Reimagined journey?

Will you choose to add your story to the thousands—the millions—of stories of curious, courageous pioneers of Life Reimagined?

Will you choose to join the Life Reimagined movement?

Things are about to get interesting.

Will you join us?

Chapter 1

This Isn't What I Was Expecting!

"This isn't what I was expecting!"

You constantly hear that refrain as people describe their response to a set of experiences in a world that is rapidly changing, a world that doesn't match the way things used to be. At the start of any conversation about what it's like to move into this new phase of life, you'll hear a long and varied list of things that people didn't expect:

I didn't expect to be divorced at my age—or to be beginning a new relationship.

I didn't expect to be unemployed—or to have the opportunity to start my own business.

I didn't expect my grown-up son to come back and live with me—or for me to have to go and live with my grown-up son.

I didn't expect my 401k to be worthless—or to have enough money to take the trip I'd always dreamed of.

What people seem to have expected is that by the time they'd reached this point in their lives, they'd have everything under control. That at a certain age, they'd have enough money, enough status, enough experience, enough stuff, that they'd have things the way they wanted them.

By now I thought I'd have this whole thing figured out.

What we didn't expect was that we'd have to keep figuring it out, no matter what our age.

Or that we'd have to deal with the kinds of unexpected challenges that, today, seem to be coming faster, more frequently, more turbulently, and less predictably.

In a world that's changing, it's time for all of us to change our assumptions, our expectations, and our mindsets of what's possible.

It's time for a new story to replace the old one.

The Old Story

For the past fifty years at least, retirement has been the single destination of living. The old story was populated by such themes as "the golden years," "life of leisure," a life without the pressure of time clocks or the demands of work. Retirement was life's desired end point; leisure time was the definition of success, the reward that awaited you after you'd put in so many years of labor. Interestingly, it took roughly fifty years for a full-fledged retirement system to find its complete expression, described by its own language and supported by pensions, policies, Social Security, and retirement communities.

As a result of that fifty-year evolution, the way we think about the path of life has been dominated by an old and familiar story. It's an outdated mental image of the life cycle that we carry around in our heads, whether we know it or not. It looks like a simple parabola, an arch that starts at the bottom left of the chart, bends up and to the right until it reaches the top, and then gradually declines to the bottom right.

The Old Story

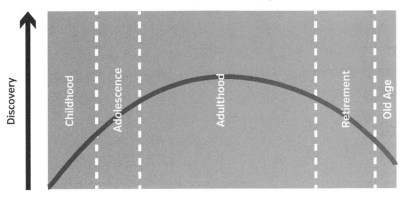

That image depicts the story most of us assume captures the reality of aging.

What it says is this: each of us starts off fresh and new, ready to learn and grow and discover our individual potential. We arc upward as we go through our early years, and we continue to grow until about the time we hit middle age. At that point we've reached the apex of our lives, the top of the parabola. After that, as we pass middle age, we begin the process of decline that takes us into retirement, then old age, and eventually, death. We've reached the end of the chart, the bottom right-hand exit point.

There are two problems with this old story.

The first problem is that the story this image tells is a disheartening, disturbing, disempowering tale. It says that the two sides of the curve of life are the same except in reverse. On the way up, we're vital, engaged, alive to learning, self-expression, and growth; on the way down, we're closed off to all those possibilities. On the way down, we're simply on the way down. We're in decline and the only question is how soon the landing will come and how hard it will be.

The second problem is that this old story is flat-out wrong. It doesn't match how we live. It doesn't describe the new reality of our lives and the lives of generations going forward. We need a new story that corresponds to the new reality.

The New Story

Imagine a new image with a different curve.

The New Story

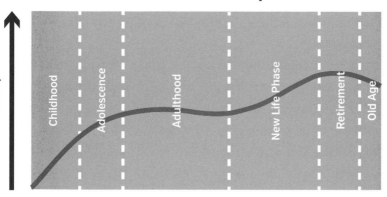

This one also begins at the lower left-hand corner and arcs upward until it reaches a point at the top. But instead of falling back down along a symmetrical curve like the old image, this one dips a little and then goes back up! It continues to rise gently for an extended period, then levels off, and finally falls at the end.

What this second image depicts is the new story about Life Reimagined.

This new story is the real story.

And it is fast becoming the new normal. Just as planning for retirement shaped the old story—and touched all of life leading up to it—this new phase will change every other phase. It is a story for the ages—all the ages. The whole of society has a stake in this story—in the new choices it offers, the new possibilities it opens up.

Just as the old story gradually assembled a system to support it, this new story will also rearrange and re-create all the components of how we live our lives. As a result of Life Reimagined, we will find ourselves, at one end of the spectrum, engaged in deep and wide-reaching policy debates touching health care, Social Security, employment and unemployment, housing, technology, and more. And at the other end of the spectrum, we will discover and pioneer new offerings and entrepreneurial solutions that touch the lives of millions of individuals with tools and techniques that transform the choices available to each of us and the pathways open to us to explore. This new story shapes a new reality, for all generations to come.

It is reshaping the architecture of society and forming one of the most significant social movements of our time.

The Life Reimagined Spiral

The best way to understand the new story is to reimagine your life in the form of a spiral, a tornado-shaped figure that starts out at the bottom and winds its way upward through a series of expanding loops toward the top. Imagine this drawing as if

Death

Birth

it were a close-up of the journey of your life, a series of twists and turns, choices and challenges from birth to death.

When you're on a flatter part of the spiral, your life is on a plateau. At those moments, things seem like they're under control. You have good work, good health, enough money, a solid base at home, a network of friends and colleagues with whom to share your life. At times like these, you may actually feel like you do have this whole thing figured out! Or at least you're satisfied with the way things are.

But then, inevitably, a trigger knocks you off the plateau; you leave the flat area and take a turn into a new zone, limbo.

What Is a Trigger?

Another word for a trigger is a wake-up call—a conscious choice or an external event that disrupts the comfortable status quo of our lives. It's a moment when the game changes, and we have to adapt to the new game.

Triggers can be positive:

> Are you in a new relationship? It's exciting, and the emotion is enough to knock you off your plateau!

> Are you launching your new startup? The challenge is enough to fill you with energy—and also to keep you up at night with exciting questions and tough challenges!

> Are you going back to school? Your calendar is now jam-packed, filled with classes to attend and homework to complete!

When you think about these positive triggers, they manifest the Life Reimagined mindset: you're exercising choice, demonstrating curiosity, and acting with courage.

Or triggers can be negative:

> Do you know someone you care about who has just heard from a doctor with an uncertain medical diagnosis? You're suddenly frozen with fear, your emotional life clouded with concern.

> Do you know people who have lost their jobs after decades of stability? They don't know which way to

turn or where to start, and you share that anxiety with them, wanting to help but not knowing how.

Do you know someone who has been caught by surprise by an unexpected divorce? All of a sudden the stability of a long-term relationship has been replaced by the unfamiliar, unwelcome experience of learning how to live alone for the first time in a long time.

These are the moments when we feel like our lives are out of control. These are the moments when we say, or hear someone else say, "This isn't what I was expecting." At times like these we wonder, "What's next?"—and the question feels like an unwelcome test, more a threat than a promise. Uncertainty and powerlessness dominate the situation. It feels like our lives are happening to us.

There are also triggers that are small and subtle, signals that add up to suggest that our lives are undergoing gradual, cumulative, and perhaps inevitable change. There are triggers that live in the gray areas of life. In some of these cases, we get to choose whether we want to accept living in the gray area or to respond to the discomfort of ambiguity and act decisively.

For example, there's a whole category of people today who are "the working worried." They're not happy in their jobs, but they're not prepared to quit. What worries them is that someone else will make the decision for them. They're working— and they're worried.

The same ambiguity applies to relationships. Not all relationships exist in the sharp dichotomy of good or bad, happy or unhappy. Many are simply in a rut. These relationship ruts aren't so bad that a breakup is inevitable, but they're not so good that they feel completely satisfying. Relationship ruts prompt the question, "Is good enough really as good as it gets?"

The truth is, we are changing all the time. Our values and priorities shift; we experience both bursts of confidence and spells of doubt; our relationships form, evolve, break apart, re-form; our work both loses energy and takes on new vitality. All of this forms an ongoing, complex life spiral.

Life in Limbo

What happens is that triggers—positive or negative, subtle or unmistakable—kick our lives into limbo, a period of uncertainty, of wondering what comes next, and of anxiously anticipating how soon whatever does come next will actually arrive.

Being in limbo is all about learning to cope with the "in-between times." As a result of a trigger, we've ended one period of stability or even one phase of life, and looking forward we don't yet see another one beginning. We're forced to live in the question "What's next?" The door behind us has closed, and we haven't seen the new doors that lie ahead. Or sometimes, although we see the new doors, we're not yet ready to make the choice to open them.

Being in limbo can be scary in the way that uncertainty often is.

And it can be even more debilitating. Limbo can become a form of resignation, a kind of prison sentence to accept the way things are as the way things have to be.

Some people let themselves fall into the trap of living the old story as if it were the new reality. You hear them say, "What do you expect from someone my age?"—a passive acceptance of life in limbo.

The truth is, when a number—your age—becomes your identity, you've given away your power to choose your future. The point isn't that sixty is the new forty. The point is that sixty is the new sixty, and there's a new way to be sixty.

Dying Without Knowing It

The worst-case scenario for those who succumb to limbo is "inner kill"—the condition of dying without knowing it. People with inner kill often feel that they either don't have enough or aren't good enough. They get stuck living in comparison with others or with some idealized, unattainable version of themselves.

You have inner kill when you've stopped growing, when you've given up on yourself, or when you find yourself always taking the easy, safe way.

Like most conditions, inner kill has a set of recognizable symptoms that let you diagnose it in yourself or someone you know: a tendency to avoid decisions; a tendency to daydream about early retirement; constant talk about intentions—without actually doing anything; not sleeping at night; sleepwalking during the day; having irritability as the emotional default setting; constantly repeating the same conversation topics week after week; making increasingly frequent visits to the liquor store, looking for a stronger alcohol prescription.

Ultimately, inner kill is the death of self-respect.

On the other hand, for those who use limbo as a moment to embrace Life Reimagined, this in-between time can be an exciting opportunity. Limbo invites a deeper, game-changing conversation with your self. You may not embrace limbo—but you can accept it, work with it, get fully engaged with the challenge that limbo presents.

Limbo is an energy crisis: if you run from it or passively surrender to it, you'll find your energy sapped. When you decide that limbo is an opportunity for self-exploration, you discover new energy and new possibilities.

Trigger in the Park

The question isn't whether we'll be hit by triggers or get kicked into limbo. We will—all of us, at every phase of life, in all kinds of ways.

The question is how we'll react when triggers come and we find ourselves in limbo. Do we retreat? Or step into the uncertainty? Respond out of fear? Or move forward with courage?

Rich Luker's story is all about overcoming fear and stepping into a Life Reimagined moment with courage. His story shows how a positive trigger can lead to realizing a new, vital, but long-deferred dream.

As a boy growing up in Ann Arbor, Michigan, Rich yearned to be able to play baseball. But he was no athlete. Small and unsure of himself, he heeded his father's expectations and stayed inside studying instead of going outside to play the game he loved.

"I was afraid on every level," Rich remembers. "I was afraid of getting hurt. I was afraid of making a fool of myself."

Still, something about baseball called to him, so much so that in college he found time to be a batboy for the University of Michigan baseball team.

"I had sports," he says, "but I didn't play. The baseball bug struck me early and stayed with me. But the thought of finding delight and playing the game never occurred to me."

Rich grew up, moved to St. Petersburg, Florida, and made his living as a researcher and consultant.

And then one day, when he was in his fifties, he found himself talking on his mobile phone on a conference call, not in his office but outside as he walked by a park. A group of men his age and older were playing softball on a diamond. The game caught his eye.

A simple game of softball served as a life-changing trigger.

"I'm holding the phone, and I'm thinking, 'What's this?'" Rich recalls. "I don't even remember saying, 'I can't talk now.' I just hung up. I'm looking through the fence and I'm seeing something I can really love. I said, 'I have to do this. I have to do this.'"

That was a Life Reimagined moment for Rich.

In that moment, he not only saw a way to do something he'd always wanted to do. He saw a way of being someone he'd always wanted to be, a way of living that he'd always wanted to experience. It changed more than the recreational side of his life; it touched every part of his life, inside and out.

In a life shaped by expectations, Rich had never expected to play softball. To be a softball player. "It was a life of watching and not doing," Rich says. "There wasn't even a realization. It's just the most amazing thing."

Today Rich still has his old job. And even after he felt that initial trigger at the park, he still had to try out for the league; he had to make a team and show he could play. But that trigger was about more than just softball. It was about exercising choice to overcome age-old expectations. It was about finding a new way to see life possibilities. And it was about shifting what mattered in life to match a new phase of life. Today, during the sixty-game softball season, Rich never schedules work between nine and eleven a.m. on Mondays, Wednesdays, and Fridays. That time is reserved for playing the game he has always loved with the new teammates he has found.

"How's that for a priority?" he asks. "How's that for pushing balance in life to say there are things more important than just work? It starts and ends with a decision to go after what you love."

Life Is Hard

When it comes to expectations, Life Reimagined says that you can find new possibilities in this new phase of life—but only if you do the hard work of reimagining. Without doing the work, there's no way forward: "If you can't get out of it, get into it!" is the tough truth of a life well lived.

Life Reimagined doesn't promise instant results or fairy-tale endings. Even the best story demands a reality check.

The problem is, some people allow their fears and disappointments, their negative past and preconceptions, to keep them from trying. They choose to live a self-fulfilling prophecy of self-doubt and disappointment.

It is true that this journey of Life Reimagined is hard. And there are no guarantees.

It's also true that succumbing to self-doubt and negative thinking does have a guarantee.

The guarantee of failure.

The Three Cs

Life Reimagined encourages and enables every individual to discover his or her real possibilities. It's a call to action, a rallying cry to do the hard work of reimagining your life.

Life Reimagined holds these three core precepts:

Choice is not a choice.
Choice is difficult. Choice is required. We are all challenged to choose, to reject victimhood, and to be choice makers. Life Reimagined is an everyday journey of making choices.

Curiosity is change.
Curiosity is the way to open up life. It allows you to see the world differently—and to see yourself differently. It kills inner kill and gives birth to real possibilities.

Courage is commitment.
Courage commits you to doing something. It requires courageous conversation and bold action, whether large or small.

Chapter 2

Get Real

Before we go any farther into the Life Reimagined journey, it's time to take a hard look at reality. Or at least what some people believe is the way their reality has to be.

This chapter is for anyone reading this book who is a skeptic. Or a cynic. Anyone who believes that Life Reimagined isn't for them or can't be for them. Anyone who dismisses it as hopelessly idealistic or impossibly romantic without bothering to give it a try. Or anyone reading this book who knows someone who matches that description.

We know people like that. In doing the research to write this book, we met them in almost every meeting. They've been in every audience and every workshop.

You know them, too.

They're the people who listen to your story about the things you're eager to try in your life and roll their eyes.

They tell you what they'd like to do—someday—and then immediately explain why they can't possibly do it today. Or ever.

They're people who respond to every opportunity, every possibility, by crossing their arms over their chest and saying, "Yes, but."

They're the people who, when they hear the Life Reimagined rallying cry, see the map and the practices, read the stories and watch the videos, immediately decide it won't work. Not for them. It isn't reality.

Get real! I can't afford that! I have to keep doing what I'm doing just to pay the rent.

Get real! I don't know what I want to do or how to choose—so how am I supposed to figure all this stuff out?

Get real! I can't make any of those moves—it would just overwhelm my wife (or husband or partner). And who needs the aggravation?

Get real! All this stuff isn't for me! It's for a small group of privileged people—and I'm not in that group!

For all those people who have all those excuses, dodges, rationales, and self-justifications, this is your chapter.

We want to answer each of those negative comments, one at a time. But first we want to tell you the hard truth. Your challenges for Life Reimagined to "get real" avoid the heart of the matter: you are responsible for shaping your own reality. You're trying to let yourself off the hook by blaming someone else—and calling it "reality."

The simple fact of life is that Life Reimagined is a reality-based approach to living.

It isn't an abstract theory applied to people's lives. It's a practical, pragmatic way to engage in life that allows anyone to take small steps toward exploring new possibilities. Which is how anyone—including you—can shape your own reality.

Let's look at those four "get real" complaints, one at a time.

Get real! I can't afford that! I have to keep doing what I'm doing just to pay the rent.

Money is hard. Period.

For many people, having enough money to keep their lives going is a struggle. They may feel like they can't fully engage with Life Reimagined until the children have finally left the house, until the mortgage is paid, until a pension kicks in.

But anyone can think about what they'd like to do—if and when they have enough money.

Anyone can do a reality check to learn more about what it would actually cost to reimagine some part of their life.

Anyone can go talk to someone who's done what they would like to do in order to learn more about the nuts and bolts of exploring a new direction.

When you look at the Life Reimagined map, almost all of it is free of charge.

Reflecting is free—and underutilized by most people. Connecting with others, sharing your ideas, learning from their experiences—that's free, too. Exploring costs you nothing. Choosing, getting more focused on a direction you'd like to get into more deeply, doesn't require spending money. When you Repack, you may even make some money if you have a yard sale and get rid of things you no longer need! Or you can cut your costs by eliminating nonessentials. Only when you Act do you run into the possibility—and it's only a possibility—that you will need to spend money.

That's how you reality-check the complaint that you can't afford your Life Reimagined journey.

The harder truth is that many people hide behind money as an excuse. Because money is so emotionally charged in our culture, money is also the first line of defense people use to explain why they can't possibly make any changes to their lives. It's the perfect avoidance mechanism.

Here are the three questions people need to ask themselves when they claim that they can't afford to do what they really want to do until they make enough money: "How much is enough?" "How badly do you want to do it?" And "What does it cost you *not* to do what you really want to do?"

Otherwise, money is an excuse, not a problem.

And that's reality.

Get real! I don't know what I want to do or how to choose—so how am I supposed to figure all this stuff out?

This is a "yes, but" response that comes from simple confusion about how change actually happens.

The truth is, the Life Reimagined approach squares with extensive research into what leads to real-world change. The prevailing notion is that the key to successful change is, first, knowing what you want to do. Then you use that knowledge to make your move. That's the conventional wisdom. And it's wrong.

In reality, change happens the other way around. Doing comes first, knowing second. As you do something—start your exploration, get out and look around, gather impressions and information—you start to know what it is that you really want to do. Doing precedes knowing, it turns out.

The notion that you have to know what you want to do before you can figure out how to do it offers people a convenient excuse for staying put, for refusing to explore possibilities, for settling for the status quo. Yet all of us are ultimately unsure of the path from where we are to where we're going next.

The reality is, you find the path by starting to walk the path.

The answer to people who say they can't use the Life Reimagined map because they are unsure of what they want to do is this: the only thing preventing you from finding out what you want to do is you. That's reality.

Here are two questions to help you get unstuck: "Starting where you are, what would be the simplest first step you could take?" And "Who is someone who could take that first step with you?"

Get real! I can't make any of those moves—it would just overwhelm my wife (or husband or partner). And who needs the aggravation?

This excuse isn't about Life Reimagined at all.

It's about the quality of too many relationships today.

Here's the reality check on this one: the majority of people feel they can't talk about what really matters to them with those closest to them. Having an honest conversation poses the biggest obstacle of all.

But burying the truth doesn't work in Life Reimagined. Life Reimagined is about freedom and responsibility; it calls for courageous conversations, conversations that tear down walls that may have been built up over years.

You may bury your feelings, but they live on, eating away from the inside.

So try a courageous conversation as a way of exploring Life Reimagined. Your partner or spouse, friend or colleague may not know what you want to do—unless you tell them. You may not know how badly you want to do it either, until you check it out.

Life Reimagined isn't a threat; it isn't a weapon to be used in a relationship. It's an opportunity. It offers you permission. If you need an excuse to explore something, to talk about something, even to try something, Life Reimagined offers you that freedom.

If the biggest fear you have is an honest conversation with the person closest to you, here are two questions to ask yourself: "Regardless of how much it might cost you to have this conversation, what does it cost you *not* to have it?" "What could you go out and do as a prelude to your courageous conversation, so that when you do have that conversation, you're talking about something you've already checked out—rather than asking for permission to explore it?"

Get real! All this stuff isn't for me! It's for a small group of privileged people—and I'm not in that group!

Let's be brutally honest: people who say this are essentially complaining that the game is stacked against them—so why bother to play?

And they're right—up to a point.

The game is stacked against all of us in different ways, some of us more than others. A reality check shows that longevity, for example, is deeply connected to education, class, and race. There are differences in the experiences and possibilities of women and men as they approach this new phase of life. That's the truth.

It's also the truth that there is always opportunity for choice.

The last of the human freedoms is to choose our way, regardless of the circumstance. For everyone who's been visited by a health crisis, a divorce, or a layoff and found themselves unable to respond to the bad news, there is always someone who has had the same harsh experience and responded by thinking that a new direction was possible. Some people respond to a problem by resignation; others treat it as a new beginning. People simply choose to handle the same experiences in different ways. That's reality.

Here's another reality check: we all live in the same questions. Nobody gets a free pass from having to confront the hard parts of life. Money, education, and status may give the illusion of immunity—and undoubtedly do provide some kinds of comfort when times get tough. But even the wealthiest among us has to answer the questions, "What gets you up in the morning?" and "What keeps you up at night?" When it comes to life's real challenges, even money can't dull certain kinds of pain.

When it comes to this issue, perception *is* reality: if you don't feel like you have a choice, you don't. If you don't bother to play because you think the game is rigged, you've already lost.

"Afraid To Take the Path"

If anyone's ever had a set of excuses for not reimagining her life, it's Barb Timberlake.

At age forty-nine, Barb still lives in the same house in Arlington, Virginia, that she grew up in. But her residence is about the only part of her life that she hasn't reimagined in the past three years.

For 26 years Barb worked for the U.S. Forest Service. While the work was secure and stable, and the agency's mission was admirable, she never felt fulfilled there.

"I sat at a desk for twenty-six years," she says, "and it was just a job. And when I walked out the door, it was gone."

She didn't know it at the time—she didn't have the Life Reimagined language to fit her life circumstances—but she was showing the symptoms of inner kill.

"I can remember walking to work," she says. "I would be trudging, always looking down. It was walking to someplace you don't want to go. Being in a box in the office was so constricting to me. I was dying away."

That was a Life Reimagined moment for Barb.

A number of triggers hit her, building on that moment, telling her that it was time—or maybe past time—for her to reimagine her life. She was significantly overweight and was diagnosed with thyroid problems, resulting in bouts of depression. At age eighty-eight, her mother needed more of Barb's time and attention. Then the Forest Service offered early retirement with her health benefits intact.

"I'd always been interested in animals," she says. "I really think I was supposed to have a career with animals. I just kept trying to figure out what it was. Was it vet school? I thought about some other things. I wasn't sure what it was."

Even while she worked in her government job, she'd been a part-time pet sitter, helping out friends when they went on vacation by looking after their dogs and cats. But she'd never thought of it as a full-time job, a business, or a way to make a living. A combination of fear and overanalyzing—thinking, not doing—was keeping Barb from exploring new possibilities.

"I think I was afraid to take the path," she says, "because it wasn't necessarily the safe path. There was a lot of the unknown. And I'm not a fan of the unknown."

She thought about the idea of pet sitting as a profession— and finally decided to do a reality check.

"It was scary," she says. "I had to think that I could really do this and earn a living. But I felt pretty comfortable that I had enough clients who love me and would be more than happy to spread the word and help me get the number of clients I need to keep my salary."

In other words, Barb's reality check gave her a new sense of reality. Rather than assuming that she could never generate enough income by pet sitting, Barb took the step of reality-checking her idea. She figured out what she would need in the way of income and what it would take to produce it.

Now her days are filled taking care of what Barb calls "all my critters"—dogs, cats, even hamsters and rabbits. And she does it on a schedule that lets her look after her own health and her mother. She takes care of the animals, and, importantly, she says, they've helped take care of her.

"There has been mutual healing," she says. "They've helped me come out of my shell a lot, and I like to think I've done some of that for them." Her whole life has improved as she re-imagined it: her physical and mental health, her relationships, her overall sense of herself. And, importantly, she has more time with her mother.

Her clients have embraced her, not only as a pet sitter, but also as a family friend, the kind of almost-a-relative who can be called on for advice and counsel in all kinds of emergencies.

"I have clients," she says, "and I'm like a member of the extended family. I've been called the second mother to some of their pets. Their kids think of me as Aunt Barb because I take care of their pet when they're not there, and they know their dog will be taken care of because Aunt Barb is there. It's really fulfilling and wonderful."

Reimagining her life hasn't been easy or simple; it's involved choice, curiosity, and courage—all three of which add up to a reality check. Along the way there's even been some humor.

"I'm allergic to just about every animal I take care of," Barb says with a laugh. "But it doesn't matter. I just take my allergy medicine."

To Barb, there's no doubt that it's all worth it.

"I really feel fulfilled," she says, "like I have finally met my purpose. I think, after almost fifty years, I have found my niche, found what I was meant to do. I have never been happier in my life. I have never felt more content. I'm out there walking a dog, going, 'I'm so happy, it's silly! This is just the best thing in the world!' I finally got my niche. And I'm in dog heaven!"

The journey to find her calling was ultimately a journey to find her self. Reflecting on her reimagined life, Barb says, "I have much more confidence. I'm much more comfortable with myself. I care about myself a lot more."

Barb's story might sound too good to be true, or too perfect to be real. The reality is, her journey was filled with tough challenges and hard decisions. In fact, one way or another, Barb had to confront every one of the four "get real" excuses. Because those "yes, but" moments happen to most people at some time.

The difference is, Barb did the work to get through them. She didn't let money or uncertainty or the expectations of others or the question of presumed status deter her. She did the work to reimagine her life, rather than fall back on the "get real" complaints as excuses to stay stuck and settle for an un-lived life.

Start Where You Are

The greatest obstacle to getting started with Life Reimagined is inertia. The only way to start is to start. That's why the Life Reimagined map is essential: a map won't make you take a journey, but it will enable you to reality-check what lies ahead.

There are no rules for getting started, but there are a few reminders to help you get under way.

Life Reimagined isn't about getting perfect; it's about getting going.

Life Reimagined isn't about setting some overarching goal. Small steps can lead to a new way of life: a tag from a child can point the way to a new diet and a life of health and wellness; walking past a public park can open up a long-postponed yearning to play on a softball team; an offer of early retirement can bring the gift of a newfound career as a full-time pet sitter and a sense of personal fulfillment.

Life Reimagined is a call to embrace what's possible, without knowing in advance what *is* possible. And without knowing whether it will turn into reality.

Life Reimagined is an invitation to reality-check your real possibilities. The promise is not that you'll find exactly what you thought you'd be looking for, but that if you begin the process, what you find may well be what was looking for you.

The promise is, if you work the process, the process will work for you. The promise is, you can shape your own reality, one step at a time.

Pioneer of Life Reimagined: Chris Gardner

Life Reimagined has its pioneers, people who, by their example, are living with choice, curiosity, and courage in this new phase of life. While it's true that we're all experiments of one, at the same time, we can learn from the stories of these pioneers. One pioneer is Chris Gardner, whose story has made him both an American legend and a global inspiration. In the 2006 movie *The Pursuit of Happyness,* actor Will Smith portrayed Chris's struggle to combine fatherhood, homelessness, and a fledgling career as a stockbroker. The story of Chris's refusal to accept defeat in his life became a film that earned Smith an Academy Award nomination for Best Actor and Chris a platform from which to pursue his own larger goals as a speaker, author, and philanthropist. Since the film, Chris's journey has changed again, to a life of inspiring countless people around the world who have the same challenges of homelessness, poverty, and parenting. Chris's second book, *Start Where You Are,* offers real-life lessons on how to get from where you are to where you want to be. He's now working on his third book.

Q: Your story combines some low lows—being homeless and trying to raise your son—and some high highs—great personal success, touching other people's lives, having your life turned into a wonderful motion picture. How do you think about choice in life compared to the things we're handed?

Chris Gardner: One of the things I'm working on in my new book is this whole concept that I call "spiritual genetics." We all understand genetics: you're going to get your mom's eyes, your dad's nose—there's nothing you can do about it.

But the spirit of who you're going to become as a man or a woman, I believe you can choose. Scientists can take a single strand of your hair, a speck of your flesh, a drop of your blood, a dab of saliva, and they can tell a great deal about you: the color of your eyes, your race, your age, your sex, any proclivities to illness or disease. But they can't tell you anything about why you became who you are. That's totally spiritual.

Q: So how would you describe your own spiritual genetics?

Chris Gardner: I had a mother who told me from the very beginning that I could do or be anything. And I believed it. That became part of my spiritual genetics.

My mother telling me as a young guy that you can do or be anything—I totally embraced that. That is what has propelled me my entire life. She did not say that you could have, you can buy, you can get, you're entitled. She said that you can do or be—and for me those statements were even bigger. Because if you can do or be anything, all of this other stuff will come. It's a matter of choosing and embracing.

Q: A part of Life Reimagined has to do with each of us finding our purpose—getting in touch with our gifts, passions, and values. How has that worked in your life?

Chris Gardner: I knew from a very early age that I wanted to become world class at whatever I did. My first ambition in life: I wanted to be Miles Davis! That's world class. I had to accept, my mother had to help me accept, you can't be Miles Davis. He's already got that job. You got to be Chris Gardner.

I had to find something that turned me on as much as the music did. And I was blessed. I found it. But it took me ten years. Something I talk about in my second book, *Start Where You Are*, is finding your button. What is the one thing that turns you on so much that the sun can't come up soon enough in the morning because you want to go do your thing, find your button?

I found mine, but it took me ten years. And when I found it, I pushed it. That's the difference. A lot of us know already what the button is. We're just afraid to push it.

Q: What was that like for you? Finding your button?

Chris Gardner: It was like reading a sheet of music! The first time I walked into a Wall Street trading room, the ticker tape is rolling, the phone is ringing off the hook, people are screaming and shouting out orders, bodies are flying all over the place. And what looked like chaos to anybody else, for me it was like I was reading a sheet of music. And I knew, this is where I'm supposed to be. Not, I think I can do that. Not, I would like to try that. This is where I'm supposed to be. I knew.

I had been looking for it for ten years. What was that one thing that gave me the same sense that I got from hearing Miles play "Round Midnight"? What was that same feeling that I got when I heard Charlie Parker blowing "Birdland"? What was that same sensation, that same energy? And the very first time I walked into a Wall Street trading room, I knew that feeling.

That's why the first thing that went into my mind was, this is where I'm supposed to be. I've been looking for this place for ten years.

Q: Another part of Life Reimagined is how each of us responds to triggers. What is a trigger in your life, and how have you responded?

Chris Gardner: The biggest trigger in my life was the recent loss of the love of my life to brain cancer. I had the honor to be Holly's primary caregiver for the last four years of her life. And one of the things that she and I talked about a great deal, the last part, was her saying and asking me, "Now that we can see how short life really can be, what are you going to do with the rest of your life?" That's a trigger.

That's the biggest trigger that I have ever experienced. What are you going to do with the rest of your life? What I had to do, I had to start taking some of my own advice. I had been telling people, I had written about it for a very long time, that if you're doing something that you're not totally committed to, if you're doing something that you're not totally passionate about, you're compromising yourself every day. I had given other people that advice. It was time for me to live it.

Q: So how has that changed your life?

Chris Gardner: Dr. Maya Angelou spoke to me many times about how, for a long time, a lot of us have been living in exile in a place called "things, stuff." And you get to a place where you realize that time is the ultimate asset.

You can make money, you can lose money. You cannot make time. Once it's gone, it's gone. Forever. So I'm not going to spend another moment, another second of my life doing anything just to make money. Anything that I do now is something that I'm doing because I am totally passionate about it and committed to it.

Chapter 3

What Works?

Here's what *doesn't* work: fear.

In the process of reimagining your life, fear is the enemy.

Fear of the past and fear of the future.

Fear of losing what you've worked so hard to gain and fear of failing to gain new things.

Fear of failing and fear of failing to try.

Fear of what people are thinking of you, or fear of people not thinking of you at all.

Fear of not knowing the right answer and fear of having too many answers.

The list of possible fears is endless—and living with fear can become a habitual way of going through life.

When you're afraid, the first reaction is to shut down your mind: avoid, evade, deny. You become closed and un-imaginative.

When it comes to reimagining your life, choice, curiosity, and courage are your allies in dispelling fear.

Reimagining is a form of self-permission: you give yourself the freedom to roam in new territories. Sometimes you're exploring within the private space of your mind, turning things over, seeing how they feel; sometimes you're stepping out into the public space of the real world, trying things out, seeing what works.

It's okay not to know exactly what you want to do next—or to want to do too many things at the same time.

It's okay not to have the one right answer—or to try many different answers to see which feels most right.

It's okay to end up in places you didn't expect to get to—or to change your mind about the place you always thought you would want to go.

It's okay to be confused or uncertain, mixed up or conflicted. It's even okay to be stuck in limbo.

About the only thing that's not okay is to allow yourself to stay stuck in limbo permanently.

So What Does Work?

As you move ahead to discover the real possibilities for your life, here's what works: having a map, working the process, and being connected to others.

Everything is open to exploration, both inside and out. Everything is an experiment, an opportunity to let go of old mindsets and past expectations, a chance to explore a new self—or several new selves—to see what fits now.

You are allowed—encouraged—to open yourself and your life up to new possibilities.

It bears repeating: reimagining your life is going to be messy.

That said, as you know from the Introduction, there is a Life Reimagined map to make sense of the territory. While everyone's life is, by definition, different, this map is a tool each of us can use.

The map won't tell you what to do, but it will help you think about what you want to do. It will help you find the right questions, adopt the right mindset, connect with the right allies, and take some of the right steps on your own personal exploration. If you take what feels like a wrong turn, it will get you back on track; if you're feeling lost, it will give you a place to come back to. It won't tell you what to decide, but it will help frame the choices you make.

The Six Practices

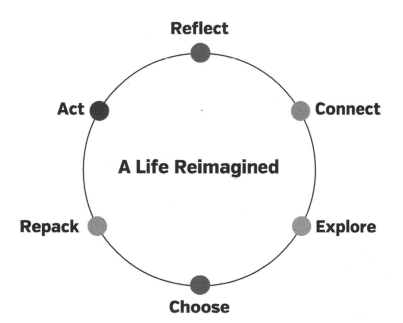

Don't confuse the map with the territory!

We each have our own territory, our own unique terrain to explore. The map is a powerful tool to help you establish your directions, get your bearings, and move ahead to new possibilities.

The map's six guideposts are a guidance system that can help each of us find our way forward. Recall what the practices are:

Reflect: A call to pause before you start the journey and then to pause at various steps along the way, understanding that change and choice occur from the inside out.

Connect: A step where you request feedback and counsel from trusted friends and guides, recognizing that isolation is fatal—no one should make this journey alone.

Explore: A beginning of the journey of discovery, a step of testing different possibilities, both inside and out, in the knowledge that curiosity and courage are essential to finding the way forward.

Choose: A narrowing of options in which you focus on your priorities and do both a deeper dive and a reality check, exploring a smaller number of choices to see which fit your emerging sense of what's right for you.

Repack: A step of deciding what's essential for the road ahead—what to let go of and what to keep, how to lighten your load, both tangible and intangible, for the new way that is opening up.

Act: A first step toward making the possibilities real is the recognition that taking action doesn't drain energy, it releases energy through the optimism that comes with choice, curiosity, and courage.

Start where you are; begin at the practice on the map where you find yourself. You may feel that you need to Connect first or that you want to Repack as your first step. This isn't a rigid, paint-by-numbers, one-size-fits-all model. You need to make it fit your own life, your own adventure, your own pace, and your own direction. Make it your own and make it fun as you try new things and explore new possibilities.

After all, you are an experiment of one.

Possibilities Journal

As you get started with Life Reimagined, following the map and working the process are the core elements. Writing in a journal will help you connect the dots of your journey. It's a way of keeping track of your thoughts, a tool for seeing and understanding your progress. A journal keeps you centered; it allows you to see fears that recur—and to recognize ones that fall away.

You can get an actual journal to write in, or you can create a Possibilities Journal file on your computer or tablet where you record your thoughts, impressions, and experiences. As you go through your Life Reimagined journey, the journal will give you a place to track your experiences.

It can be as simple as an idea file, a place to put lists of movies you want to see or books you want to read as you re-imagine your life. It can be a list of new people you meet as your journey evolves. It shouldn't trigger writer's block; you shouldn't feel that writing in your journal has to be a dreaded homework assignment with a grade attached.

However you use it, a journal will be an important tool for you as you explore Life Reimagined.

A Talking Journal

If writing in a journal doesn't work for you, try adopting as a daily ritual "a talking journal." Every day, check in with a close friend, a colleague, or your spouse or partner for an informal chat. What issues are pushing you? What opportunities are pulling you?

Regular conversation can clarify your thinking and offer a path for breaking through to broader ways of reimagining your life.

Here's an exercise you can try: pick the partner you want to have as your "talking journal" companion. For seven minutes, you do all the talking. Your companion is not allowed to interrupt, ask questions, or make comments. His or her role is to listen in absolute silence.

You may start out making small talk. It may take some time for you to reach the truth point. But before too long, you'll find yourself talking about something that is important to you, something below the surface that is trying to come out. After seven minutes, switch roles: your partner does the talking, you do the listening.

Often people who do this exercise find themselves saying something they've never said before—not because they didn't want to talk about it, but because they felt no one was listening. Sometimes you don't know what you're thinking until you hear yourself say it. This exercise enables you to practice courageous conversations by playing the roles of both truth teller and deep listener.

Getting Started

For many people, making the first entry in a journal can be a daunting task. Putting the first words onto a clean sheet of paper feels like a test, as if the wrong opening can ruin everything that might come next.

Here's an easy way to begin your Possibilities Journal by starting where you are.

On the first page, write down your name.

Write down the date.

Write down your location. It can be where you're sitting, or it can be where you're living. But locate yourself for yourself.

Write down something about what you're doing. How do you spend your time now? What is your occupation or vocation? Describe yourself as you are now.

Finally, look at the Life Reimagined map. Where do you locate yourself on the map? Are you at Reflect? Connect? Explore? Or are you at Choose, Repack, or Act? Write down in your journal where you place yourself on the map today. Mark your entry point for your journey.

That's it. You've started your journal—and your journey—simply by locating yourself in the present.

Now go read one of the next six chapters in this book, the one that corresponds to the practice where you've placed yourself on the Life Reimagined map. You're on your way.

Pioneer of Life Reimagined: Emilio Estefan

Emilio Estefan's life story is an almost perfect fit for the Life Reimagined map. It's as if he has already taken the Life Reimagined journey and can tell the rest of us what it feels like.

Emilio's is a life that began in poverty in Cuba, then took him to Spain as a boy before he arrived in the United States to discover the amazing career that was waiting for him. Over the course of his life, Emilio has been one of the most successful, prolific, and generous musicians and producers in the entertainment world. The winner of nineteen Grammy Awards, he has also developed and directed the careers of many of the music industry's most celebrated Hispanic superstars, including his wife, singer Gloria Estefan, as well as Jon Secada, Ricky Martin, Jennifer Lopez, Marc Anthony, and Shakira. In 2008, Emilio produced and directed a full-length documentary film, *90 Millas*, telling the story of the pioneers of Cuban music. In 2010 he released his best-selling book, *The Rhythm of Success: How an Immigrant Produced His Own American Dream.* Among Emilio and Gloria's many philanthropic activities are the Gloria Estefan Foundation and the Miami Project to Cure Paralysis, an outgrowth of a 1990 bus accident that left Gloria temporarily paralyzed. Now the royalties of three of Gloria's songs will go to the Miami Project to Cure Paralysis in perpetuity.

Q: Did you always know what you wanted to do? What your life would be about?

Emilio Estefan: I knew all my life, even when I was a kid, I wanted to be a musician, a writer. Coming to Miami, I told my uncle, "Let's go, I want to see an accordion." I went to a place, and we found this accordion. It was like $177. And the guy said, "You can make payments, like $17 a month." I said, "Let's do it. Don't worry about it."

My uncle said, "How are we going to pay for this?" And when we got to my aunt's house with the accordion, she looked at me and said, "How are you going to pay for this?"

And I said, "Don't worry! I will find something to do with this and that will make some money."

What I did, I went and I applied at a restaurant. I used to work at Bacardi at six in the morning, go to school in the afternoon, and at night I used to go and play the accordion for tips. That's how the whole thing started.

But you know something? It's having to find what you love in life. And I think I knew all my life when I was a kid what I wanted to do in life. I knew that music was the most important thing in my life and I found that.

Q: One of the key parts of Life Reimagined is the idea of discovering new possibilities in your life at any age. It seems like you've always lived that way.

Emilio Estefan: My life has been that all the way from the beginning. It started being a musician, being a writer. Then I became a producer. I became a director. I became a businessperson. We also opened restaurants. We have almost 4,000 employees, and ninety-five percent of the people have been with us for almost thirty years, and I think that's key.

The key to my life is, even if my life was very negative when I was a kid, I convert the whole thing to positive.

When you're going to get to sixty years old, you have to do what you love.

Some people want to relax. Some people want to keep working.

Myself, I want to keep working until I die.

I was a kid who came to the United States with a lot of dreams. I'm lucky enough to live in the best country in the world, where every dream came true. It was hard because, being a Latino, when we came, it was really hard to sell something that people were not familiar with. But we were very persistent about the sound.

At the same time, every decade you have to reinvent yourself and you have something new. But when you get to almost sixty years old, one thing that you've found is experience. It's a balance in your life.

Being creative and having the motivation to wake up in the morning and do things that you love. It makes the whole difference. And it would make a whole difference in the world if people would think that way.

Q: A lot of people find it hard to make decisions about their lives—what to let go of, what to pursue. You've had to make hard decisions since you were a young boy.

Emilio Estefan: It was hard for me to leave Cuba when I was eleven years old. I became a man thinking that I have to get my family to live in a free country.

I remember when I arrived in Spain. I was only fourteen years old, and we arrived in Spain at around ten o'clock at night with not even a sweater. No jackets or anything because we were coming from Cuba. And I walked a long corridor, and at the end it was two priests waiting for us to take us to the shelter.

And the minute I came out of the airplane I was crying because, of course, I said I left. I made a big decision. You are fourteen years old.

My dad told me, everything will be okay. We made the right decision. You're going to live in a free country.

Forty-five years later I came back in a private plane with a lot of success. I start walking the same hall and I tell Gloria I have to stop for a couple of minutes.

It was the same hall that I walked forty-five years ago.

And you know something? When I saw my daughter smiling and my son smiling and having such a great time—I made the right decision.

So, in life you have to make decisions that sometimes are hard, but at the end you have to make decisions to keep always going in the right direction. I think a lot of things that I did in my life, I did it for the right reason. Because I love to work. I love to live in a free country. I love to live in a place that I feel that I'm not only going to earn my living, that I can give back to the country. And I think we accomplished that.

Q: One of the most traumatic experiences that you and Gloria have had to live through was the bus accident in 1990. That was a huge trigger that altered everything in your life. What did you learn from that difficult time?

Emilio Estefan: I think the accident changed a lot in our life. When we went through this incredible accident with Gloria, you realize that fame and money, you can lose it overnight. And the only thing that you leave to other people is what you do to help them, what you do to help a whole community.

What happens when you get into an accident like happened to us, the first you think is, why me? Life is not fair.

But even from the bad moment that we experienced at that time, we learned so many things. How to give even more back. How to tell people that you love them when you have to tell them, because you don't know what is going to happen to you.

When they told me that Gloria was probably not going to be able to walk, I fainted. I cannot register the amount of pressure that I was feeling at the time.

At the same time, when I saw Gloria telling me our kid is alive, it changed the whole moment about the accident. Even if I was paralyzed or whatever happens, my kid is alive. A lot of people, they lose their family or they lose their kid or their wife.

Even if it was a hard thing for us, and Gloria having to learn to walk again, we went through so much in life, but we learned a lot of things.

How to appreciate life. I always tell people I live my life as if it's the last day I'm going to live. When I do an album, it's like the last album I'm going to do. Or it's the first album that I did, with the same feeling. That feeling that you say, oh my God, I want to put one hundred percent of my life to do this album.

I think we learned a lot of things in many ways, and it's going back to zero. When that accident happened, we went back to zero to restart our whole life again. And then we enjoyed even more the concerts. Every concert that we did after that, it was like a joy. Every concert that we did and performed all over the world, it was a blessing.

I think you realize that sometimes you have to go through hard times to appreciate life. And we were lucky enough to learn from that experience.

Everything in life has negative and positive things. And we learned a lot of things having that accident.

Q: Life Reimagined says that no one should go it alone—that we all need to connect with others to realize the real possibilities in our life. How does that apply to you?

Emilio Estefan: I would never have been able to do anything, of course, without my marriage and Gloria, and besides that all the people who have worked with us who have been key in our careers. My friends, the people who have been with me since I started, people that I see like they were family. Key people, for example, Quincy Jones, who is like a part of our family, helped us when we were starting and gave us a point of support, telling us that what we were doing was right. You have to be surrounded by incredible people, by people who you pass on your thoughts to and your happiness that you have about what you have. I don't think you can ever be able to do things in life by yourself.

Chapter 4

Reflect—What's Real for You?

If you talk with people in the latter part of their lives and ask them to look back on how they've lived, you'll hear a consistent refrain: "If I were to live my life over, I'd be more reflective." Dig a little deeper, and they usually add, "Happiness is a choice, not a result of how life treats you."

What they're really saying is, reflection is all about *choice*.

What is reflection?

First, let's dispel some misconceptions. Start with what it isn't—and what it *doesn't* require you to do.

Reflection doesn't require you to go off to a monastery. You don't have to light candles and learn to sit in the lotus position. Soothing music isn't necessary; you don't have to practice chanting or learn a mantra. (To be fair, these may be helpful practices for some people; they're just not required.) The point is, it's not an esoteric experience designed to make you self-conscious—at least not in an uncomfortable way.

But you do, actually, want to become more conscious of yourself—in a good way.

Reflection is about pausing to look at life from the inside out. It goes back to the Life Reimagined Spiral. In trigger moments we tend to do two things: we go higher, and we go deeper.

"Higher" means we lift our heads to take a hard look at what's going on out there that might have caused the trigger. Why did I lose my job? What's behind my relationship crisis? What have I been doing to trigger this health problem? Going higher is what we do to get more information from the environment to make sense of the moment, positive or negative.

"Deeper," on the other hand, is when we go within. We start to turn the questions inward. What are my choices? What are my real possibilities?

When you go inward, you begin to discover what's essential. It's when you learn what's core for you. Going inside gives you the chance to discover what doesn't change about you, no matter how much change is going on outside in the world. It gives you a chance to record the things in your life that are nonnegotiable.

Going deeper gives you a chance to take the Life Reimagined manifesto and make it personal: What are *your* choices? What are *you* curious about? What are *you* ready to act courageously on?

It's Your Time

Reflection is a break. Think of it as a mini-vacation from the daily business that absorbs most of our time, too much of the time. Reflection is a chance to get in touch with yourself, to go inside and listen to yourself.

For many people who have spent their lives taking care of others' needs—raising a family, looking after parents, paying the bills, taking responsibility for outside concerns—reflection is a welcome pause, a chance to take some time for themselves.

It's your time to explore yourself.

Each of us has a story, a narrative of our life. Part of reflection consists of telling yourself about yourself—of revisiting your own story, the narrative in your head about your life up to this time. But the point isn't to extend that narrative into the future unquestioningly. The point is to examine that story and then to use it to reimagine what's possible going forward—to use the threads that are the through-lines of your past to weave a new story for the future.

Getting To Know You

Reflection might start with culling your past experiences, looking at what worked and what didn't work in your old story. Then you see what you might want to pull forward into your new story in this new phase of life.

It's not that the old story is "wrong"—it simply no longer works, or no longer works as well as it once did. Reflection lets you look at the "in-between moment": a time between the old story that is familiar and a new story that is unfolding. It's a choice point, a Life Reimagined moment.

Reflection is a time to ask yourself questions about how you use your time. Do you reserve your time for things that matter to you? Are you more loyal to your past? Or are you forming a new, powerful loyalty to what you want to have happen in your future?

Reflection also serves a particularly useful purpose for people who have an impulse to charge ahead—who just want to get on with it. Sometimes that instinct to "just do it" is a clue, a suggestion that it would be a good idea to slow down, hit the pause button, and do a little stocktaking before moving forward. Otherwise the old story may take you in a direction that you don't really want to go in—or that you may regret after you take it. You may be acting out of habit and familiarity rather than reflecting on new possibilities.

If Only

How many times have you thought or said, "If only"?

If only I'd known then what I know now.

If only I'd followed a different path.

If only I'd married a different person.

If only I'd bought that stock when I had a chance or taken that job that was offered to me, or moved to that other city, or acted on that hunch.

Hindsight is always easier than foresight. Which is why it's always tempting to rely on hindsight as a crutch instead of working at foresight through reflection.

Wouldn't it be great if you could see ahead into the next phase of life to make the choices that would work out better? Wouldn't it be great to know what the wiser path was in advance, so you could follow it? Foresight can't guarantee you a "right" answer—as if there were such a thing. But it can give you a way of reflecting on new possibilities that come from within your core self.

The problem with living in hindsight is that it leads to an

identity based on "used to be." It leads to being stuck. We've all had the unpleasant experience of being stuck at dinner or on an airplane, sitting next to someone who's living in hindsight, someone who "used to be" someone—but who isn't anyone right now. They're not living in the present or the future; they're not living who they are now or creating who they could become.

Simply replicating your past is a prescription for inner kill. Repetitive patterns deaden your curiosity. They anesthetize your emotions and numb your senses.

Reflection means resharpening your curiosity. It means exploring the future, using curiosity and courage as tools for foresight.

Reflection is when hindsight and foresight come together. It's blending the story of your past with the possibility of your future.

Fulfilling Time, Not Just Filling Time

Reflection begins with a new relationship with time.

Without reflecting on your real priorities and new possibilities, you're on autopilot. The excuses—too much work, not enough money, too many responsibilities for others—won't fly when you recognize that you own your own time.

Time is your most valuable currency. Are you satisfied with how you're spending your time? Your life? When was the last time you went to sleep at night, content with the feeling that "this was a well-spent day"? When was the last time you got up in the morning, clear about how you wanted to spend your day?

Reflection helps you say no to the less important things that simply clutter up a life and yes to the more important things that define the purpose in life.

Life Reimagined focuses on *fulfilling* time, not just *filling* time.

A Pizza Epiphany

If you were to walk into Paulie Gee's pizzeria in Brooklyn, New York, you'd probably think that the friendly, outgoing middle-aged man who's running the place had been doing this all his life.

You'd be wrong.

"I was masquerading as a computer geek," Paulie says, looking back on how he spent his life before he opened up his own pizzeria. "I wasn't a geek, but I had a job where I had to appear to be one."

As a young man, Paulie had done what many people do: he'd listened to the advice of his parents and taken a safe path—but not the path that matched his own gifts, passions, and values. "My father grew up in the Depression," Paulie says. "My parents told me to get a good civil service job, and that's what I did."

Then the usual things in life came along in the usual way— a house, a mortgage, the responsibilities for earning a living and paying the bills.

"I couldn't change if I wanted to," he says. "I had a career that I wasn't really suited for. I grinded it out. I thought, you pick a career, you work, eventually you build up a retirement fund, you retire, and you go do something you like."

He knew that a trigger was approaching, that his life was going to change. But he wasn't sure exactly what was going to happen, how it would change, or what would come next.

"I had a freight train coming at me," Paulie remembers. "I always knew in the back of my mind that there must be something I'd really enjoy. I kept on looking for it. I love to cook, I love to entertain, I love music and to play music for people."

In his own way, Paulie was already reflecting on his own story, on the through-lines from the past that he might weave into a new future. He was going deeper inside, while at the same time keeping himself open to the possibilities that might present themselves from the outside.

"Then I discovered a place in Coney Island called Totonno's. It was my pizza epiphany!" he says. "I went there and I was really blown away!"

That was a Life Reimagined moment for Paulie.

Taken with the distinctive taste of pizza cooked in a coal-fired oven, sparked by his own curiosity, Paulie began to explore the world of pizzerias and to meet the pizza gurus in New York. It was challenging, he saw, but it seemed like something he could do. Next he learned about pizzas cooked in a wood-fired oven.

"Eventually," he says, "I said, this is something maybe I could do. I said, I'm going to build one of these ovens. Once we bought the bricks, that was it! I decided, I'm going to open up a pizzeria."

Paulie knew that he would need to learn more if he wanted to act on his choice; he'd have to practice, experiment, and improve his pizza-cooking abilities. Here again he chose to do it his own way: through more exploration.

"I didn't go to a pizza school and pay thousands of dollars to get pizza lessons," he says. "I did it myself."

He experimented with new recipes for the dough, tried different combinations for the toppings—all the time exploring what it meant to make great pizza, getting more information and a clearer idea of what would work.

Then he had to find a place for his pizzeria, a community he wanted to join.

"I was in love with North Brooklyn," he says. "There was something going on. It was new, it was a vibrant neighborhood, and I wanted to be a part of it. I found Franklin Street, and I was smitten. I knew I was home."

From that pizza epiphany, Paulie Gee has created a whole new way of working and living.

"I've found something I can do for the rest of my life, and enjoy it," he says. "That's happiness."

Take Time To Make Time

Everything starts with time.

It's one of the oldest and wisest truths of life: *you have to take time to make time.*

There's something about taking time to reflect that teaches you how to live better. Reflecting is the ongoing and continuous practice of making your life your own.

Reflection opens up hope. It's not always a reaction to a sense of disillusionment or frustration. It can be a proactive process, something you do at each step along the path, a way of examining what has brought you this far, evaluating what worked and what didn't work, and imagining what's possible. And it can be something that happens in an informal way—a short pause in the middle of a busy day when you give yourself a moment to reflect on something you saw, something you heard, something you thought.

The truth, however, is that for many people reflection doesn't come naturally or easily, particularly in a life filled with busy-ness and outside demands. It's hard for many people to create the time for reflection. They may not know where to start or how to begin.

Start with a Life Checkup

To get started with reflection, go to the Life Checkup on the Life Reimagined web site (www.lifereimagined.org). This easy exercise is a powerful tool for you to engage with the Reflect guidepost. It's not the kind of exercise you do once and never revisit. Just as you have an annual physical with your doctor or a regular visit with a financial advisor, the Life Checkup can become a regular and reoccurring part of reflecting on your own journey. Use it to check in with yourself yearly, perhaps on your birthday.

After you have taken the Checkup, go to your journal. What choices did the Checkup suggest? Did the Checkup make you curious about anything new? Are there actions you should consider as a result of the Checkup?

Simply by taking this annual life exam, you may discover themes that help you imagine a new way forward for this new phase of life.

Chapter 5

Connect—Who's There for You?

Throughout life, community is important. In this new phase of life creating a sense of community is essential. It's the expression of connection.

It's so self evident that most of the time we take it for granted: humans are social animals. It's in our DNA—literally. We've survived and evolved because of our innate capacity and need to connect with our fellow human beings. We're not meant to live solitary lives. Talking, listening, touching, and relating are hardwired into what it means to be human. Connecting creates a sense of well-being for all of us in every phase of life. We need to depend on one another for all kinds of things, from specific lessons that teach us how to do something better to more general emotional support in dealing with the triggers that are always a part of life.

But here's what happens to community and connections over time: they tend to fray. Think about it.

In the early phases of adulthood, we often make connections and form communities around two spheres: family and work. It's a common experience for many people who have children: the children become the reason for community and connections. The friends you make, the associations you join, the school games or performances you attend, all derive from your children and their interests and development. That's a powerful connection, one that brings people together around a shared commitment to their families. Your friends are the parents of your children's friends.

Of course, not everyone has children; often, when that's the case, the extended or blended family creates the connective tissue. Family get-togethers at holidays or special events help build a feeling of belonging and community.

The second zone where we make solid connections is around work. The intensity of the experience in the workplace brings people together. Colleagues at work have to learn a new language, take on external competitors, overcome shared obstacles, and collaborate for a common purpose.

That's all pretty obvious and ordinary.

What's not so obvious is that it's also ordinary for those connections to fray as we move into this new phase of life. *Very simply, the original reasons for the connections may no longer apply.* Forty years later, the parents of your children's friends are less likely to be your friends. You may have simply moved apart socially as the original basis for the connection has lost its importance. You moved to another city—or they did—and you've lost touch. The social glue—and the reason for it—has come unstuck.

The same is true for work. You may have changed your job, lost your job, or retired from work entirely. The good old days may give you a reason for an occasional lunch date or a cup of coffee with colleagues from the past. But the energy that came with hard work over a sustained period of time begins to dwindle as the actual work experience becomes a distant memory.

The reality in this new phase of life is that it's all too easy to end up with a wealth of casual acquaintances and a poverty of real friends.

And that is likely to happen at the exact moment when we all need authentic connections to help us do the new work of reimagining our lives—and helping other real friends reimagine their lives.

One way to think about the step of connecting is that it involves two dimensions: the outer work is about creating community; the inner work is about finding authenticity.

Isolation Is Fatal

We live in a country that has a deep cultural strain, one that values individualism and a go-it-alone mindset. And we live in a time when geographical mobility and social separation have made it all too easy for people to have fewer meaningful relationships. You can have hundreds of friends on Facebook and not even know the name of your next-door neighbor. As a consequence, people try to solve dilemmas themselves, either because they think it's a heroic stance to take or because they are acting out of a feeling that they don't have anyone close to talk with. The fact is, the burden of going it alone is heavy and limiting—and potentially dangerous.

When social scientists look at the effects of being isolated or feeling isolated, their findings confirm what we all know from our own experiences: *isolation is fatal.* In fact, social isolation can take up to seven years off of your life. Isolation contributes to heart disease and depression; it influences your immune system and leads to faster aging and advanced health problems.

The antidote is community, or connectedness.

The hunger for connection holds true for both men and women—although women seem to do better at connecting. Which may explain why women live, on average, seven years longer than men.

New Kinds of Community

In this new phase of life, making and having real friends and finding a valued "family" that you connect to are essentials in the journey of Life Reimagined. Part of what it takes is reimagining the kinds of relationships that matter. In the new phase of life there are more opportunities for creating different kinds of family and friendships than existed in the past.

"Family" doesn't mean only the family you were born into. You can form close relationships in this new phase that feel like family, even if they don't fit the traditional definition. And you may find yourself thinking less about having one mate who shares your life and more about having "mates"—good friends who genuinely get you and offer you deep friendships that don't necessarily involve living together.

You can see examples on college campuses where housing is being built, not for entering freshmen, but for older adults. These older learners may have retired, or they may simply want a new lifestyle that involves continuing education and intergenerational connection. Other experiments involve the co-housing movement, a new form of communal living for people in the new phase of life.

The goal is to create a new kind of community, one where people live independently but have a shared support system. They have the feeling of family without being related or living under the same roof. The aim is to discover places and people that help make connections.

The bottom line is, there are no rules and few role models that apply to these new and emerging categories for connecting. We're free to innovate, create, explore.

Hunger for Authenticity

The reason Connect comes after Reflect in the Life Reimagined map is that, after we go inside, we often need others we can talk with about what we're thinking, feeling, and discovering. No matter how authentic the conversation you have with yourself about yourself, it runs the risk of covering the same ground, over and over, with no new insights. You recycle the same ideas and revisit the same obstacles that you've been carrying with you from the past. It's hard to see with fresh eyes when you're the only one looking at yourself.

The truth is that as you reimagine your life, others may see you more clearly than you do. And others may have more courage for you than you have for yourself.

Someone else can listen to your reflections and offer you support on how to knit the pieces of your life together—or how to unravel them when necessary. And it's a two-way street: you may be a committed listener for a close friend who wants to get your perspective on his or her reflections. These are connections that create community, fight isolation, and offer encouragement to reimagine life with authenticity.

A Good Question Beats a Good Answer

Often the Life Reimagined journey presents itself in the form of questions: At this point in my life, what gives me energy—and what drains me? What are the deep and persistent tugs in my life—the pulls toward something that won't leave me alone until I address it? What doors in my life seem to be closing—and what doors are opening? In dreams, what images present themselves that suggest a direction I may not be ready to acknowledge consciously? What direction feels right—even if there are no hard data to verify it? If I pay attention to surprisingly recurrent signs or suggestions, what direction do they seem to be pointing to?

Life Reimagined requires you to live in these questions. But there is a risk. Questioning yourself about something that others around you might deny, take for granted, dismiss, or be too uncomfortable to address could lead to isolation. Their attitude—"Get real!" "What's your problem? Are you having a midlife crisis?"—may belittle or dismiss the value of this time of self-reflection.

When that happens, connection is all the more important. Having one or more committed listeners overcomes the denial or disinterest that could discourage you from doing the Life Reimagined work that leads to hope.

Here's another important dimension to this step in the journey. What you want in a good listener is not someone who will offer you an answer to the questions you're asking your-self, but someone who will deepen and magnify them. A com-mitted listener holds up a mirror so you can see yourself with more clarity. A good question beats a good answer—especially if the question connects you to the gap between what you have in your life and what you want from your life.

Acceptance and Connection

Before she could connect with her purpose in life, Annie Walker had to connect with herself. In fact, acceptance and connection have been the through-lines in her life story.

"I always had a dark cloud over my life," she says. "It wasn't until after I started writing poetry that I could totally embrace who I was. It just happens that I'm gay."

She had had a son, Jason, one year after she married at sixteen. She was so young that people assumed her son was her brother.

"My son grew up knowing me as his buddy," Annie says.

At the same time, her son had a hard time accepting her for who she was, at least at first. "Then he wrote a note to me in a card," she says, "later in life, after he started maturing. He said, 'Mom, as long as you're proud of who you are, I will al-ways be proud of you.'"

Jason was diabetic, and even though he was diagnosed very early, he had his own issues with accepting his condition. He developed high blood pressure, then kidney problems that ultimately cost him his life.

In the wake of her son's death, Annie again turned to the intersection of acceptance and connection.

"It wasn't until recently that I've been able to cope with Jason's death," Annie says. "It's only through a real love group that I attend that I was able to realize and embrace the fact that I was angry with him for dying because he died so young and I felt so cheated."

Jason died in February, 2005. Six months after she lost her son, Annie lost her job.

"That night," she remembers, "when I went to bed, I was unable to sleep." She found herself lying in bed, listening to the clock tick, looking for direction from God and the universe, knowing that there was a path for her.

That was a Life Reimagined moment for Annie.

"It all came together," Annie says. "I had to start over. I was a high school dropout. I did obtain my GED. I went to the City of Phoenix Workforce Connection. They had a program that would help pay for my college."

While she went to school, she worked for different home health companies, sometimes 60 or 70 hours a week. The combination of learning and working was hard but rewarding.

"It all had purpose," Annie says. "It all had meaning."

Her own life experience gave her a heartfelt appreciation of her patients and a connection with them—what they were going through, what they needed.

"I have a connection with my patients," she says. "And I'm able to connect on a level that they're not threatened at all. They feel they can trust me—and they can."

Now that Annie's fifty-five, her Life Reimagined journey has taken her from reflection to connection—and beyond.

"My job and what I do, it honestly feeds my soul," she says. "It's what I'm meant to do. I know that I can go to work and I can make a difference. I can change a life."

Now that she's embraced acceptance and connection, Annie feels a sense of possibility for what lies ahead.

"Who knows where the road is going to take me?" Annie says. "There is not an end in sight. The future is just open."

Don't Go It Alone

While the journey belongs to each of us alone, the key is not to go it alone.

Like Annie Walker, most of us can trace our successes to pivotal support from other people. Sometimes the support is indirect, even distant—a role model who may not even know that she offers inspiration. Other times the help comes from a mentor who decides to offer hands-on support that makes all the difference in opening up new opportunities.

Think about your own life story. In your Possibilities Journal, answer these questions:

What are the important connections and relationships that have sustained you along the way, particularly in times of transition?

Who are the people today you can rely on for wise counsel or outside inspiration?

Who gives you feedback that you can put to good use?

Who helps you resist the temptation to shy away from the discomfort that accompanies hard questioning and deep personal reflection?

Who's There for You?

This is where a Sounding Board is essential. A Sounding Board is a small group of people whose only goal is to help you get what you want. A Sounding Board helps you reimagine what's next; it's a solid resource for you to use during times of transition. Sounding Boards are catalysts for change.

You can build your Sounding Board around five friendly acquaintances—or find one committed listener who offers you the kind of support you need. You can build a long-term board that helps you over a sustained period of time—or you can make up a Sounding Board to help you address one immediate issue.

The best boards contain a diverse group of people, each of whom plays a different role: a *committed listener*, who holds up the mirror; a *catalyst*, who helps you get outside your comfort zone; a *connector*, who plugs you into other resources, people, and learning opportunities; a *task master or trainer*, who holds you accountable for doing what you say you're going to do; and a *mentor*, who helps you keep your eye on the long view and the big picture.

Your Sounding Board members can come from many walks of life, but it helps if they have specific knowledge or experience with the category of life you want to address: work, relationships, money, health, or all of these. Each board member must pass the Life Reimagined litmus test: *do they get you?*

They have to care about you rather than wanting to cure you. They must be deeply interested *in* you, rather than wanting to be interesting *to* you. They must be able to ask great questions without presuming to know the answers.

In your Possibilities Journal, write down names of people who meet these criteria:

> Do they care about me? Are they less interested in judging me and more interested in supporting me?

Am I comfortable being transparent with them? Am I open to having courageous conversations with them?

Are they committed listeners? Do they ask great questions?

Do they get me? Are they willing to live in the questions with me? Are they compassionate?

Your board should be clear enough to you in your own mind that you could convene imaginary meetings and have imaginary conversations. You could even have a deceased person on your Sounding Board—perhaps your late mother or father, whose wisdom you respect—and have an imaginary conversation where you ask yourself, "I wonder what she would say about this choice?"

Almost as important as figuring out who you need on your board is being clear about who you don't need. You definitely don't need people who are naysayers, who are consistently pessimistic, or who won't take the time to listen. You want people who have a bias for action. To reimagine, you need to overpower the forces of procrastination.

Ultimately, a Sounding Board will hold you accountable for action so you overcome excuses and cold feet.

Start today by selecting *one person* who could make a difference to you. Ask whether it would be okay if you checked in with him or her every few weeks or months to share your progress and to be held accountable. Finding the right people is more important than worrying about where they live. You can use technology to stay in touch. A Sounding Board member can be in another city, state, or country.

When you invite individuals to be members of your board, you need to clarify your expectations: what's in it for them, what's in it for you. Don't overlook the value of their time; their time and input are precious commodities.

And remember: connection is a two-way street.

You may ask someone to be a member of your Sounding Board. Or you may find people asking you to be a member of theirs. Connection works both ways.

Pioneer of Life Reimagined: James Brown

James Brown—J. B. to his fans and friends—is a true team player in sports, work, and life whose public career and private life embody what it means to connect with others. He is one of the most respected sportscasters and sports journalists in the United States. As the host of *The NFL Today* on CBS and *Inside the NFL* on Showtime, J. B. brings knowledge, perspective, humor, and humanity to the world of sports.

After an outstanding college basketball career at Harvard—and a short-lived tryout with the Atlanta Hawks of the NBA—J. B. went to work in business, taking positions at such companies as Xerox and Eastman Kodak. He began his career as a sports broadcaster in 1984, doing Washington Bullets television broadcasts. His compassion and integrity were on display in 2009, when he interviewed NFL quarterback Michael Vick on *60 Minutes*, the first time Vick had spoken publicly about his criminal conviction and prison sentence for dogfighting. In addition to his work in sports, J. B. is an ordained minister and community counselor, meeting and praying with people from all walks of life.

Q: Part of Life Reimagined involves the way each of us looks for our own purpose in life, combining our gifts, passions, and values. How do you think about your own purpose?

J. B.: I think my purpose is one that is still evolving. In a very general sense it revolves around helping, assisting, encouraging, strengthening, contributing to a sense of community. Certainly a lot of my work life has been involved in team-oriented pursuits. And that's probably because it started that way in the nuclear family, being the oldest of five kids. So it's always been about team with me, and team is all about helping the others on that team so that we collectively are successful.

It truly does take teamwork to make a dream work.

Q: Another important part of Life Reimagined is the idea that we all encounter triggers in our lives—events or experiences that knock us off a plateau and make us adapt to a new situation. What triggers have played a role in your life?

J. B.: In terms of my life as a whole, there were at least three significant triggers that I can recall. One was in elementary school. I wanted to be a doctor. I'll never forget getting the book that I checked out of the library. It was called *So You Want to be a Doctor?* And I was excited about it. But I remember there was a teacher in the fifth or sixth grade who said, "Well, you know, little kids like you don't do well in math and science, so you probably shouldn't consider being a doctor. You might want to consider being something else."

That was a very important marker in my life because I realized that what you say to a kid—and actually, for that matter, to anyone—can have a lifelong impact. And you always want to be encouraging.

Q: That's a terrific example of not only how a trigger hits you, but also how you learn from it and what you do with it. What was the second trigger?

J. B.: The second trigger was when I was in junior high school. The coach could see I had a lot of raw talent, but I wasn't good. I wasn't a polished act at all. But that junior high school coach saw how hungry I was to learn, that I paid rapt attention to what he was saying, and therefore he selected me to be on the team, even when there were clearly people who were more polished than me. But he really liked the fact that I hung onto his every word and that I was going to take what he told me and go to work on it.

So that was another trigger. But when I got to college I got complacent, rested on my laurels, didn't work as hard to stay on top as I did to get to the top. Come senior year and the NBA draft—and I wanted to play professional basketball because I knew that was my destiny—I got drafted by the Atlanta Hawks. I knew I could make this team. I knew I could play, but come the last day of camp, the coach was calling me to talk with me. And I'm thinking he's calling me to compliment me, and he says, "I've got to cut you. I'm letting you go."

I sat there and wept like a little baby, because I knew I had the talent to make it.

But as opposed to pointing the finger of blame at somebody else—I remember our bishop telling us, if you're pointing the finger of blame at somebody else, there are three pointing right back at you. I thought about that, because I couldn't point a finger of blame at anybody else, because I realized that I didn't work as hard to stay on top as I did to get to the top.

At that point I made a firm decision that I would never, ever allow an opportunity to pass me because I was ill-prepared.

Q: Another positive life lesson from what must have been a very hard, negative trigger. And your third trigger?

J. B.: The third trigger, and the most significant trigger in my life as I got older, was and is the faith foundation. There were some real voids in my life. I was a young fella, dressing nicely, single, tooling around in a little sports car, having a great time, going to happy hour.

But you know what? There was a real emptiness in my heart. I remember driving up this long road late at night coming back from a club, and I said, "God, I know what's missing in my life. It's You. If You will come into my life, I will commit myself to Your way."

It was not until I asked Jesus Christ into my life and to have him guide me and submit myself to him, that everything else fell into place. That was the third, most significant change in my life in terms of that faith foundation, that faith component that has helped me along the way that I'm pursuing now.

Q: Go back for a moment to your family, your sports career, your own purpose. What do you think the lesson there is?

J. B.: Once one becomes more enlightened, more aware, more attuned to what success is all about, it's never a solo pursuit. It never is. And even if we use the examples of sports—tennis is a solo sport—it's not that player alone. It's that player's coach, the tennis coach. It's the conditioning coach. It might be the nutrition coach. It might be the one who motivates him. It's always a team pursuit. Make no mistake about it.

Q: What is the core of Life Reimagined for you?

J. B.: Life Reimagined is about recognizing that there are passions in you, there are gifts in you that don't have an expiration date at all. You ought to make certain that you fully maximize that and engage and give back so that you are a meaningful contributor in your own community.

Chapter 6

Explore—What's Possible for You?

It is by many accounts the greatest advertising campaign in business history—certainly the most iconic.

If you don't remember it or never saw it, it starts quietly with a few subdued notes from a piano and a black-and-white video image of Albert Einstein.

Then we hear a voice, simple, honest, direct, authentic: "Here's to the crazy ones," it says. "The misfits. The rebels. The troublemakers."

The images on the screen advance with strength and elegance: Bob Dylan, Martin Luther King, Richard Branson, John Lennon and Yoko Ono, Buckminster Fuller, Thomas Edison, Richard Feynman.

"The round pegs in the square holes," the voice says evenly. "The ones who see things differently. They're not fond of rules and they have no respect for the status quo. You can quote them, disagree with them, glorify or vilify them," the voice calmly tells us as the parade of iconic faces continues.

Muhammad Ali, Ted Turner, Maria Callas, Mahatma Gandhi, Amelia Earhart, Alfred Hitchcock.

"About the only thing you can't do is ignore them. Because they change things. They push the human race forward. And while some may see them as the crazy ones, we see genius."

Martha Graham, Jim Henson, Frank Lloyd Wright, Pablo Picasso.

"Because the people who are crazy enough to think they can change the world are the ones who do."

And then the two words that capture the message: *Think different.*

The year was 1997, and the company was Apple.

But it could just as easily be today, and the commercial stand as an ad for Life Reimagined.

Because all the people featured in that advertisement were explorers. They lived their lives on the outer edge of curiosity, not the inner edge of security.

That's what this next guidepost, Explore, is all about: thinking differently about yourself.

Because the people who are crazy enough to think they can change their lives are the ones who do.

With exploration, you begin to change your journey; you begin to open yourself up to the unknown. You begin to separate the old story—what you've always done, who you've always been—from the new story—what you'd like to learn to do, who you'd like to become.

With exploration, you disregard the old voice in your head. The one that says, "I can't do that!" The one that tells you, "That's not who I am!" The one that says, "Get real!" or "Yes, but." The one that keeps you from trying new things, from stepping outside of your comfort zone, from giving free rein to your curiosity.

Curiosity—exploration—is what you use to push yourself up the new life curve, rather than allowing yourself to slide back down along the old slope.

You Don't Know If You Don't Go

The beauty of exploration—and the power—is how simple it is to do.

You let go. You let go of preconceptions and prescriptions.

You explore without having a reason to explore.

You accept the unknown. You tell yourself, "You don't know if you don't go." And then you go.

Exploring is brainstorming with your life: there are no bad ideas. Exploring is your conversation with a new set of possibilities, a new set of likes and dislikes.

Pick one of these activities, try it out, and then write about it in your Possibilities Journal:

Go to a local newsstand and intentionally buy and read a handful of magazines you've never read before—and that previously never appealed to you. If you like science magazines, buy a publication with short stories. If sports is your regular read, take home a cooking magazine.

Next time you're on a drive, get off the freeway and take a side road. Or if you've got a regular route home, take a new one.

Let yourself go to a local tavern that features country and western line dancing every Friday night—even though you've always told yourself that you can't dance. And that you hate country and western music.

Try one of these explorations—or one you design yourself—and then write down how it felt in your journal. Did it provoke any new ideas? Did it make you question anything you've taken for granted? Was being outside of your comfort zone something you could get better at—maybe even learn to enjoy? How does it feel to be in a situation that is a little scary? Do you tend to seek new information—or shy away from dealing with ideas that are unfamiliar? The point is to practice the art of exploration simply to see how it feels when you do it.

Exploration is a journey of discovery—and by definition, you can't take a journey of discovery if you already know everything about your journey.

The problem is, most of us don't like uncertainty; we're uncomfortable with not knowing. So we shy away from danger and flinch in the face of risk.

We are more comfortable with things we're already good at than we are with opening ourselves up to learning new things—and remembering what it feels like to be incompetent as a learner.

But think about the actual journeys you've been on. The moments of spontaneity are what we remember from the trips we take. They're what separates an adventure from just another trip.

Life Reimagined encourages each of us to be the explorers, not the knowers. It encourages us to go and discover what surprises await us.

A Formula for Exploration

Go back to that Apple ad for a minute. What do all those people have in common?

Yes, they were all geniuses in one way or another. And they all lived their lives with choice, curiosity, and courage.

But they also embodied a formula for life that not only defines their spirit but also characterizes the possibility of Life Reimagined. It's the formula for exploration.

The formula is: G + P + V.

G stands for gifts. It's where you should begin when you're exploring a choice, a change, or a possibility. What are your strengths? How can you explore using them?

P stands for passion. Ask yourself, "What do I care about?" "What needs doing in the world—or in my community?" Consider putting your gifts to work on some area of need that you care about.

V stands for values—how you see yourself operating in the world. What lifestyles and work styles fit your style? Your temperament? Your values?

When the elements of the formula G + P + V are in alignment, you live your best life. You're using your gifts on something you believe in, and your environment supports your effort.

Comfortable with Being Uncomfortable

At six feet, seven inches and 310 pounds, John Drury is hard to miss. And as a combination truck driver/dance instructor, he's even harder to ignore.

"I'm a truck driver and a dance fitness instructor," he says. "I think I'm the only person out there that does this."

He was tipping the scales at 400 pounds when he was picked to compete in a local "biggest loser" contest in Cincinnati. His cousin had died young at age thirty-seven, and

John saw the pain his cousin's family had suffered. It was a trigger for him to look after his own health.

That was a Life Reimagined moment for John.

But driving a truck made that hard.

"The truck driving lifestyle is brutal," John says. "No two ways about it. You might go on three or four hours of sleep, night after night. You only have so long to stop and grab something to eat, and it's usually fast food."

The contest gave him free use of a gym, and the gym introduced him to the Zumba fitness routine, a workout based on dance.

Dance and movement were things John had always loved. A passion long banked started to be reignited.

"I love everything about dance," John says. "It's a passion—mind, body, and spirit. When I was younger, growing up, as far as dancing goes and my curiosity is concerned, it was the neighborhood I grew up in."

Break dancing was part of the scene; everyone would get out and do their thing, showcasing their dance moves out on the street. For John, it was more than a passion; he had a genuine gift for it.

John began by exploring Zumba, rediscovered his old love of dancing, and started teaching fitness his own way at Big John's Dance Fitness. His diet improved: no more fast food, no more soft drinks. He lost one hundred pounds. Now he drives his eighteen-wheeler during the week, then comes home to teach his classes on weekends.

"Dancing is my calling," John says. "Dancing is me. I'm the size I am, six feet seven inches, 300 pounds, and nothing is going to slow me down, nothing's going to stop me."

His calling extends from improving his own health to trying to encourage the obese to improve theirs. It's where he brings his values into the equation.

"Just because you're obese doesn't mean you're not human," John says. "You still have feelings. You still like music, and want to get off the couch and move a little bit."

John knows that he can serve as a role model for all kinds of people who might not believe they can lose weight, get into shape, embrace a healthier life style.

"I'm on this journey with my students, with my pupils," he says. "I'm not there yet. They walk into my class and they say, 'If this guy can do it, I can do it!'"

Having gone on his own journey of exploration, he wants to encourage others to take the same path. "That's what I'm trying to tell people: step out of your comfort zone," John says. "Start to be comfortable with being uncomfortable."

If John's size and energy and enthusiasm don't convince his students, one look at the side of his shaved, bald head might get the message across. There he sports a tattoo in script that says, "The old me is dead and gone."

Having come this far, John is eager to continue to explore whatever lies ahead.

"Age has nothing to do with it," he says. "I feel like I'll be in my seventies doing dance classes."

Life at its source is about exploration. Outer exploration is a function of inner imagination and passion.

For some people passion is a dangerous word. It connotes a loss of control.

But passion also means freedom, the kind of freedom that is life-affirming and liberating. As John Drury discovered, tapping into your passion can be a way to discover your calling. It unleashes new possibilities and opens up your life to new opportunities.

You may not think you know what your gifts, passions, and values are. Or you may not have the language, the name for your gifts, passions, and values. You may need some help to see them through a different lens, a way of viewing them that lets you bring them into the world—the way John Drury's gift, passion, and values morphed into a calling for fitness instruction. And from there, to helping others.

What's Calling?

Calling Cards (on the Life Reimagined web site: www.lifereimagined.org) is an exercise for you to explore your G + P + V formula. The exercise invites you to sort a deck of fifty-two cards into the things you most enjoy doing. Each card represents a gift—a strength or a talent. Within the deck are six suits that represent the way you like to operate in the world: Realistic, Investigative, Artistic, Social, Enterprising, Conventional. You look at each card, then sort them into three piles: "Yes, that's me"; "No, that's not me"; "I can't decide." Then you look at the "Yes, that's me" pile and pick the five cards that you most identify with. You take those cards and see which of the six suits or categories they most fit into. Ultimately, the exercise gives you paths to explore as you seek to take your gifts, passions, and values into the world.

It's a fun, playful way to uncover or give a name to your own story, an exercise that will help you uncover your gifts— even the ones you may have forgotten.

Chapter 7

Take a Break—Whew!

Time to take a deep breath. Stretch. Relax for a minute.

If you've ever gone backpacking, you know that it's a good idea to pause by the side of the path when you're roughly at the midpoint of your adventure. Put down what you're carrying; check what's in your bag; test the weight of the load; make sure you've got the right supplies with you—and that you've gotten rid of things you don't really need.

It's a chance to look back and see the ground you've already covered. You get to assess the choices you've made: do you still want to make the journey? You can test your curiosity: does this path seem interesting? And you can evaluate your courage: are you committed to keeping on this path?

That's what this brief chapter is about.

If you sense that the first three practices—Reflect, Connect, Explore—on the Life Reimagined map go together, you're right. There's no requirement that you travel in a straight line; you can zigzag and choose your own way of moving around the map. But if you did do them all, you should be in a position now to consider where you've been and what you've done. You should have notes in your journal that track your progress, capture your experiences, and trace your thinking. And you should be well prepared for the next three practices that lie ahead.

By starting with Reflect, you've entered the Life Reimagined journey, not by rushing out into the world, but by going inside, into your own self. You've taken a step back from the busy-ness of daily life. Perhaps for the first time in your life—or the first time in this new phase of life—you've given yourself permission to take some time to look at who you are and what you want.

If you went to the web and took the initial Life Reimagined Checkup, you've begun to learn more about yourself. If you watched the Paulie Gee video about his pizza epiphany (which you'll find on the web site), you've seen that Life Reimagined is for all of us.

Reflect helped prepare you for Connect. When you learn more about yourself, it gets easier to look for travel partners—others with whom you can share the journey. With each step along the path, you become aware of new choices, new curiosities, and new ways to act courageously. Each step gives you renewed energy for the rest of the journey.

The practices that were part of Connect should give you a strong foundation from which to move forward. Creating your own Sounding Board is an essential step in the Life Reimagined journey. We all need other people who can see us with fresh eyes and help us frame our choices with different points of view. You'll find yourself coming back to your Sounding

Board at every stage of your journey as you go deeper into the possibilities and choices that you encounter along your path. If you watched the videos of Annie Walker and James "J. B." Brown, you saw how powerful Connect is for all of us as we take the Life Reimagined journey.

It stands to reason that with new insight from reflection and new support from connection comes the curiosity and courage to begin to Explore. If you did the Calling Cards exercise, you'll have gained a clearer picture of your gifts, passions, and values. Taking them out into the world to explore what they could become is a step that should be liberating and fun, a chance to begin to try out new possibilities that, perhaps, you'd never considered before. John Drury's video shows you what can happen when you embrace and develop your gifts.

You don't have to lock into any specific choice—that step is yet to come. Importantly, when it does come, you'll have gained more self-awareness, more support from others, and more deep-seated appreciation of your own self. These are capabilities that will equip you for the next three guideposts on the map—Choose, Repack, and Act—where you begin to make some clearer choices, select what you need to take with you on the next phase of the journey, and finally act on your choice.

Okay, our brief pause is over! Time to resume the journey!

Chapter 8

Choose—What's Next?

Life Reimagined says we make better choices—and find fulfillment—when we live from the inside out.

Think about it this way: at its core, life consists of choices that involve having, doing, and being.

The way the old story encouraged people to "pursue happiness" followed this logic: If I *have* enough—usually money—then I'll be able to *do* what I want—but have delayed choosing—and then I'll finally *be* happy.

The new story flips that process: you start with *being* yourself, with who you are authentically. That leads to *doing* things that are in alignment with who you are. Finally, as a consequence, you *have* a fulfilling life—one that is both successful outwardly and feels authentic inwardly.

In the new phase of life, getting this process right is an urgent task.

Go back to the Life Reimagined stories, the people you've met in earlier chapters. One of the most striking points is what these explorers and pioneers *didn't* say.

No one mentioned making money to buy more things.

No one mentioned a life of leisure or luxury, a life of taking it easy.

No one talked about cashing it in or walking away from life to do their bucket list.

No one talked about comparing their lives to the people around them—who had more money, a bigger house, a fancier car. They didn't measure their lives against someone else's.

And no one talked about the old story in which retirement was the default destination.

Every one of them said, "I can do this for the rest of my life!"

They consistently made choices that gave them a healthier and more fulfilling life—a life that allowed them enough "having" and a lot of "being."

When it comes to choosing, the path is clear: choose fulfillment.

How To Choose Fulfillment

Remember at the beginning of the book, when we told you that life transitions can be scary—and that's okay? When we said that Life Reimagined isn't a pat and easy answer, a cut-and-dried formula that you follow in a cookie-cutter fashion?

With the guidepost Choose, we've reached one of those scary places.

Up to now, the Life Reimagined map has encouraged you to go inside, to connect with others and to open yourself up to new possibilities by open-ended exploration.

Now with this step, it's time to narrow your direction to a few choices.

For some people, the act of choosing feels scary.

What if I make the wrong choice?

What if I get in over my head?

What if I commit to a path that, when I get into it, really doesn't suit me?

If that's you, relax! The kind of choosing you do at this point in the Life Reimagined journey isn't that all-or-nothing kind of commitment.

At this point, what Life Reimagined suggests is that you begin to get more specific about ways you could take what you've learned about yourself and bring those gifts, passions, and values into the world. And there may be many different ways to do that—it doesn't have to be the "right" one.

Choosing is still part of exploring, but it involves winnowing down your options to fewer possibilities to achieve greater clarity. And it requires more courage—the courage to walk through one or more of the doors that you've discovered through exploration. You're still trying out options—different versions of your reimagined life—but you're beginning to narrow the options and go deeper into a few of them.

Small Bites, Easily Chewed

Reimagining your life doesn't have to be scary, but it does require serious intention and the willingness to take some small steps. With an emphasis on the smallness of the steps.

Choosing doesn't commit you to an irrevocable decision. Instead, choosing is about small bites that are easily chewed. Remember the old joke: how do you eat an elephant? The answer is, one bite at a time.

The same goes for choosing at this point in the Life Reimagined journey. You don't have to swallow the whole elephant. You just have to take a first bite—and then another, one bite at a time.

You can make the act of choosing easier and more palatable if you break it down into small rituals that you do with regularity. When it comes to Life Reimagined, you're only as good as your practices—the work you do. Rituals make practices a regular part of your day; they become fun, easy, a source of pride and a reminder of the progress you're making on your journey.

Rituals can be as simple as *pause, reflect, act, and learn.*

For instance, one small ritual is to make regular appointments with yourself and put them on your calendar. This is a pause, a time that you set aside to use for your Life Reimagined work, a time when you can't be interrupted. No phone calls, no emails, no knocks on the door. Take a technology fast. You set aside time to examine your options, to think, read, write, and imagine different possibilities.

Another ritual should be reflecting on a regular basis, taking time to write in your Possibilities Journal as well as going back to review what you've written in the past. The point is to write things down that you want to capture, things that will help you find the clues that will help you choose.

You can also make it a point to take simple actions every day, actions designed to give you more information and to teach you new lessons. As you refine your choices, for example, check out people and places that are engaged in the things you're curious about. Visit organizations that give you insights into the field you're interested in. Volunteer to spend time in a place where the choice you're interested in is being played out. Shadow someone who is doing what you think you might want to do. Then record your reactions to these investigations in your journal.

Make it a point to check in regularly with the Life Reimagined web site to see what new videos, apps, exercises, and stories have been posted to deepen your own journey.

You want to be ready every day. Ready to learn, to listen, maybe even to choose. It will make every day more valuable, more exciting—and your life more fulfilling.

What Are You Going To Be When You Grow Up?

Everyone knows that there's no business like show business.

But we don't all know what it's actually like to be in the business of show business.

"Broadway, particularly, is very, very repetitive," says Tripp Hanson. "You do it eight times a week. It is a schedule for tri-athletes."

Tripp should know: as a pianist, singer, tap dancer, and actor, he was a veteran of five Broadway shows, including such smash hits as *Kiss Me Kate* and *Thoroughly Modern Millie*. That was before he became an acupuncturist.

The question for Tripp wasn't success; it was too much success and the simple truth that, over time, the work got harder and harder to sustain.

"Forty did not feel like thirty at the end of a show," he remembers. "And there was a sinking, sick feeling. What if I'm not going to spend the rest of my life doing what I set out with such gusto to do?"

But knowing that you want to explore doing something new, and knowing what that something might be—or even how to discover it—those are different things. In Tripp's case, part of the answer came from revisiting interests and notions he'd had as a boy.

"When I was a kid, if you asked me, 'What are you going to be when you grow up?' from the time I was four years old, I would say, a doctor," Tripp says. "I was intent on this idea of becoming someone who would help people get better."

As it turned out, the line between Tripp's old interest and his new calling wasn't a straight one—or a predictable one.

"I had a dog," he says. "Mr. Spanky. Spanky was having trouble with his knee. It was so bad he stopped coming down the stairs. Somebody said to me, 'You should try doggy acupuncture.'"

Doggy acupuncture? Tripp's reaction was, "They do that for dogs now?"

But eventually he took his pet into the acupuncturist for two treatments.

"I came in the house one day," Tripp remembers, "and Spanky went right down the stairs!"

Seeing his dog move without pain gave him pause.

"I have this thing with my foot," he thought. "Maybe acupuncture would help that."

His first appointment was eye-opening.

"He put this needle somewhere on the side of my leg and all of a sudden it felt like this whoosh," Tripp says. "I felt this rush of energy and it was almost like a tiny little firecracker went off in my foot. I asked my acupuncturist, 'How does this work?'"

That was a Life Reimagined moment for Tripp.

It was more than an acupuncture treatment; it was a clue for Tripp to consider, a new door he might want to walk through, a new way to explore an old interest.

"Here we go," he says, "the old 'I want to be a doctor.'"

But if he really wanted to look into a new direction, he'd have to do more exploring, and eventually, commit to a new direction.

"I was sitting in the dressing room of *Thoroughly Modern Millie*," Tripp says. "And I was saying to the guys, 'Where do you study acupuncture? Do I have to go to China?' They were saying, 'There's a clinic on Fourteenth Street at the Tristate College of Acupuncture.'"

His choice of direction meant he enrolled in classes, testing out the fit between "being that kind of a doctor" and his own gifts, passions, and values.

"Chinese medicine ultimately made sense to me," he says. "And this medicine has just enough theater to it for me."

When he thinks back to how he found his way to acupuncture, Tripp offers the advice of someone who knew he was looking but wasn't sure what he was looking for.

"Things are going to grab your attention," he says, based on his own experience. "Pay attention when they do. And when the challenges arise, that's when we learn who we really are."

He's embraced a new path, but without completely letting go of the old one. "I still go pull out my tap shoes every now and then and take myself into a studio and work up a little sweat tap-dancing," Tripp says. "That part of me is not dead, it's not gone. It's just part of a larger picture now."

And as for his new path as an acupuncturist, one who

counts Broadway stars among his patients, Tripp is very clear about the rewards. "Love is a big thing for me," he says. "Loving what I do, love being, feeling engaged in what I do."

At this point, Tripp is being, doing, and having a life he loves.

Goals and Purposes

Who gets to choose?

For too many people, someone or something else has made the choices for them. Their parents, their mortgage, their boss, their friends, the demands of life. They may wake up, 20 or 30 years down the road, stuck in a job, a career, a marriage, a city or town that they never actually chose, wondering how they got into it—and how to get out of it.

With choice comes opportunity and responsibility.

If you want to reimagine your life, you have to be the one who chooses. You get the opportunity to do it, and you accept the responsibility for the outcome.

That said, there is a difference between this step, Choose, and the one that comes later, Act.

Choosing is part of the process where you start to test different possible ways to apply your gifts, passions, and values. But it isn't yet making the commitment to one specific way.

The difference between choosing and acting is like the difference between having a purpose and having a goal. A goal is a specific result that you want to achieve, like losing 10 pounds. Purpose is the "why" behind the goal.

The difference between the two is time. To reach your goal you set a deadline: I'm going to lose ten pounds in the next three months.

Purpose isn't about time—it's about direction. It's broader, deeper, and longer. Instead of thinking about losing 10 pounds in three months, think about leading a healthier life—the deeper reason behind your goal of losing weight.

At this point in the Life Reimagined journey, you're still not acting—you're not yet ready to set a specific goal with a concrete timetable.

You're still narrowing your options, but not yet committing to any one of them. You're matching your purpose to possibility.

In making that match, you can listen to your gut, trust your intuition, check your feelings against what the outside world is telling you. And you can embrace ritual, using daily practices to fine-tune your sense of what's right for you and what's possible in the world.

Either way, choosing is a part of the Life Reimagined process to find greater fulfillment.

Chapter 9

Repack—What To Lose, What To Take?

Everyday experience tell us that we're going through a time of unprecedented changes: changes in the economy that make life harder; changes in medicine that make life longer; changes in lifestyles that make life more interesting.

Life Reimagined responds to those external changes. And it goes beyond them to something deeper and different.

Life Reimagined is about more than changes. It's about *transitions.* And while we often use those two words interchangeably, they don't mean the same thing to us or demand the same thing from us.

Think about it this way: change is often situational, factual, external. You change your job and move from one line of work to another. You change your address and move from one town to another. You change your status in life and move from single to married or back again. These are the kinds of changes that can show up on a tax form, a driver's license, a résumé.

Transitions are personal in a way that can't be captured on

a government form or job application. Transitions, compared to changes, have a deeper resonance, a more elemental quality: they're not about what's out there, they're about who's in here.

Transitions ask us to come to terms with changes. Transitions are about who we've been, where we've come from, and where we're headed. They ask us to look hard at what we've collected along the way—both tangible and intangible—and to jettison the baggage that no longer fits who we are or who we want to become. Transitions are about the inner repacking and reimagining we have to do in order to make the most of the change that's going on in the outside world.

Transitions—and the art of repacking—have to do with the gradual falling away of the old and the equally gradual emergence of the new.

Repacking is an essential part of making meaningful life transitions. Without repacking, you don't actually make anything new happen in your life. Repacking simultaneously helps you get "unstuck" from the past and helps the transition you're making to the future actually "stick."

Repacking is the step we take when we figure out what to keep and what to give up or to give away. It's the process we use to come to terms with letting go of the way things used to be and to embrace the way things are now or will be as we move forward.

A Life of Stuff or the Stuff of Life?

Whether we know it or not, all of us are collectors.

When we were kids, we might have collected baseball cards or Barbie dolls, matchbook covers or stamps.

As adults, we collected other things—sometimes consciously, sometimes unconsciously, sometimes tangible things, sometimes things that were intangible. Much of this had to do with the combination of roles, costumes, and acts that we tried on in the course of our lives. A career that required us to dress a certain way meant we collected the clothes that went along with the job—and the attitude to support it. A fascination with a hobby turned into a collection that reflected that interest and a personal story that revolved around it: flies, rods, and reels for trout fishing; cookbooks, kitchen tools, and cutting boards for cooking; tents, sleeping bags, and backpacks for camping. If we're avid readers, we collect books. If we're photographers, we compile collections of pictures. If we love to work with our hands, we collect tools.

One way or another, what we do is to collect stuff. Stuff can be tangible items and artifacts that decorate our homes. Stuff can also be memories, dreams, regrets—experiences and emotions that decorate our inner lives. Stuff can be habits, beliefs, ways of communicating, ways of relating to others, or a self-image that we've carried with us for years.

The stuff we collect, if we're honest about it, comes to represent who we are—or at least who we've been. It reminds us of the jobs we've had, the interests we've pursued, the people we've connected with on the journey of life up to now. For some people, their record of jobs, titles, and positions comes to stand for their life—or even deeper, their identity, how they think of themselves. For others, family photo albums filled with old pictures of kids raised, vacations taken, holidays celebrated, validate the way they've spent their lives.

There's nothing wrong with being a collector or having your collections.

But there's everything to be gained by taking a hard look at all this stuff. And to ask yourself this repacking question: what are the essentials for the next phase of my journey?

Am I just *filling* my life with stuff? Or am I going after the *fulfilling* stuff of life?

The process of repacking gives you the opportunity to take a hard look at the stuff you have and to evaluate it.

It transforms the tangible and intangible things in your life into a deeper question of identity and possibility: Am I still the person who collected all this stuff? Are these the things I want and need as I emerge into this next phase of life? Are these old things and old habits of mind holding me back and weighing me down? Would I be better served by letting go of some old things to make room for some new ones?

Repacking Time

Like other steps on the Life Reimagined journey, at its core repacking has everything to do with time.

In the new phase of life, a heightened awareness of time shapes every guidepost on the map—but none more powerfully than Repack. When we Repack, we make a conscious effort to differentiate time, separating the past from the future. In the process, we also weigh what's essential and what's unessential.

It's also true that when we reach midlife and beyond, we're more acutely aware of the limits imposed on us by time.

Maybe now is the time to say no to obsolete demands, attitudes, and commitments from the past in order to make time for the yeses that are waiting in the future. Maybe now is the moment to resign from committees or boards that no longer hold meaning for us. External validation or social approval no longer hold much sway—not when time is what matters. And it's *quality* of time that counts: what matters is fulfilling time, not filling time.

As we move through life, we're much more likely to confront the inescapable reality that no one lives forever. Mortality stands near the center of every Life Reimagined story. Life Reimagined reminds us that we are all creatures of time. We live in time, and we all belong to time.

It's not a new awareness, or even an original observation. Wisdom traditions, religions, philosophers, poets, artists, and songwriters have all made the point for a long time.

The question is, how do we use this awareness? How do we make the wisest choices about how to spend our limited time? How do we make the most of each day?

Repacking is the practice that offers a powerful approach.

To repack is to look carefully at what we're carrying: what's absolutely essential for the journey and what's not.

To repack is to decide what to lose and what to take. It is an expression of choice, curiosity, and courage. It is a practice that challenges you to lighten your load.

To succeed in this new phase of life, we need to learn to pack, unpack, and repack often. That takes asking the right questions, questions that are represented by the practices on the Life Reimagined journey: Reflect, Connect, Explore, Choose, Repack, and, ultimately, Act.

By asking these questions and seeking the deeper understandings they prompt, we are assured that we will keep moving forward with energy and creativity.

"Why?" Is a Dangerous Question

When you repack you take a long, hard, honest look at what you're carrying and why you're carrying it.

Which means that repacking makes you confront the basic question, "Why?"

Why do I get up in the morning?
Why do I do the work I do?
Why do I live where I live?
Why do I buy what I buy?
Why do I want what I want?
Why do I have what I have?
Why do I love who I love?
Why do I keep what I keep?
Why do I think of myself the way I think of myself?

"Why?" is a dangerous question. It offers freedom at the same time that it demands responsibility.

As soon as you ask "why?" you open up the possibility of choice.

That's one reason why Repack is one of the hardest, most demanding, and most important steps in the Life Reimagined journey. It's also why Repack is the next to last guidepost, the practice that comes just before Act.

Repack asks you to go back through each of the prior steps in the journey—to revisit the previous practices and to think about what you learned at each step along the way.

You go back to Reflect, to see if what you said made sense to you and to match your reflections with the baggage you have in your life compared to what you told yourself mattered.

You Connect with your Sounding Board—and with your

own inner voice that helps you measure the life you've led up to now against the life you aspire to going forward.

You Explore to examine once again the options you've been weighing, the possibilities you've discovered and that life has presented you—and to select what you will need to move ahead with what appears to be the most fulfilling choice.

You Choose the paths that feel most right to you—and get serious about jettisoning the costumes and roles that helped define the old you in order to make space for the new you that is in the process of emerging.

Repacking—asking "why?"—takes deep choice, curiosity, and courage. You may ask why and decide to stay with what you already have, what you're already doing, who you're already being. Or you may answer the question by undertaking to Repack your life and make room for a new set of choices.

Repacking is the step in the Life Reimagined journey that calls upon us to confront the underlying proposition at the heart of this new reality: choice in life is imperative.

Not to Repack—to shrink in the face of this challenge—is to fail to grow into your authentic self and to discover the real possibilities that lie ahead for you.

The way to grow is to step into the new and emerging possibilities presented by Life Reimagined. To enable that to happen, you have to be willing to let go of things from the past—the old you—that are no longer relevant to the person you are becoming.

Repacking On Purpose

Sometimes people repack their bags because they want to pursue a new direction.

Sometimes, on the other hand, repacking comes at the end of a gun.

"I was the eldest, and my sister and brother were cornered," Maria Vasquez remembers. "One of the militia was holding a machine gun to us. That's how bad it was."

The year was 1959, and Fidel Castro and his Cuban revolution had just taken everything normal from a young girl's life and her family's circumstances.

"There's a word—*destierro*—and it means, when they rip you from your land," Maria says. "It's not something that you leave because you want to. It's because you have to."

Her father was put in prison under the Castro regime, jailed because of his political beliefs. "The militia, people dressed in green, the people from Castro came into our house and they came to harass our family," she remembers.

The choice that presented itself was to flee, to come to the United States, and to leave her father behind.

"We left right when the revolution started," Maria says. "It was our chance to grow up in freedom."

But getting to Miami with her mother, brother, and sister didn't guarantee an easy time.

"It was like a big question mark," she says, remembering what it felt like to be separated from her father and to start a new life in a new land. "When will we ever see our father? Would we ever see him again?"

Starting over required her mother to begin again from the bottom.

"My mother was always very positive, very strong, very hardworking," Maria says. "She always taught us to look forward no matter what happened. She had a PhD in philosophy, and when we came to the United States, the only work she could find in the beginning was as a maid in a hotel." To save bus fare, her mother would walk to and from work each day.

Then word came: her father had been released from prison by mistake! He and some friends were able to hijack a boat and make it to Miami. He was in Key West—and a short time later Maria's father was home, the family reunited.

No matter where she lived, Maria remembered the flavor of life in Cuba. For a while, she and her husband were living in Venezuela, and they found themselves thinking back to the good things that made up the cuisine of Cuba. What if they tried to bring those tastes to people who no longer lived on the island? What if they started a business of selling Cuban food—over the Internet?

That was a Life Reimagined moment for Maria.

"We were over 50 years old when we started," Maria says. "And this for our generation was a business where most people don't even know how to handle a mouse! So it was difficult to do that. But we started from home and it started growing. We started shipping all over the United States and then we started shipping abroad to Europe."

They opened up a retail business, a store filled with the smells and flavors, roots and traditions of the Cuban lifestyle. With their Internet business, Maria and her husband were able to ship huge volumes of Cuban goods all over the world.

"What I love about what we're doing with this store is putting my country out there," Maria says. "Showing people who we are. Our store and our business have become an icon of the Cuban culture."

For Maria, repacking her bag—literally, on that fateful day

in Cuba—has led to a life that is a demonstration of what each of us can do when we reimagine our lives.

"I believe that I am at the peak of my purpose in life," she says, "the purpose of showing people that life is what you want it to be. Happiness comes from inside. Life outside might give you instant gratification. But happiness you have to find inside yourself. If you do not have a purpose, you cannot have happiness inside of you."

It's Not That Simple

Repacking is not merely about simplifying your life. That can be part of it, but there's more. And sometimes simplification oversimplifies what's really at stake.

When you're at a trigger point, handy solutions can be tempting. The stress and anxiety that accompany a trigger make easy answers look good: Downsize. Move. Quit. Leave. Just simplify your life.

The problem is that simplify-your-life strategies don't address the underlying reasons your life feels so overcrowded—or empty—in the first place.

Repack is more than a simplification strategy. It takes you deeper into the core of "Why?" Why do you have the things you have? Why do you do the things you do? Why do you feel the things you feel?

As Maria Vasquez's story illustrates, if we have a "why" to live, we can bear almost any "how." Repacking is all about the why; it's a way to make the step forward, the one that leads to Act.

So don't confuse repacking with merely simplifying.

That said, simplifying your life *can* be a good, useful, and even fun starting point. By having less *in* our lives we can often find ways to get more *out* of our lives.

Repacking means getting rid of the clutter of life, the stuff that's irrelevant to our purpose and fulfillment. It involves choice. It requires a deliberate reimagining of our lives for the sake of a purpose.

That's the power and utility of repacking.

The fun comes with the practice. And with the application of a little imagination to the actual repacking of our bags.

For example, give yourself a small, manageable, but real exercise: clean out a drawer or a closet to see what repacking feels like.

After you've done this simple exercise, write about it in your journal. What did you decide to give away? What did you decide to keep? And why? How does lightening your load help you move faster, easier, smoother?

Another exercise for your journal: When you think about repacking for your Life Reimagined journey, what kind of bag or backpack would you choose? Do you still need that old briefcase, or is that a carryover of a person you once were but are no longer? Do you want a suitcase—or a backpack? Let yourself have some fun with the process. Your chances of finding the way forward increase with the amount of fun you have in taking the trip.

Repack Your Self As You Repack Your Stuff

Repack represents an essential step in moving to the next phase of your life. But knowing that doesn't necessarily make it feel better or easier or more comfortable.

Transitions can be hard. All transitions start with an ending, move to a period of limbo, and then lead to a new action or a fresh beginning.

But endings rarely come without some pain, a sense of loss, a feeling of sadness. Endings mean letting go of something—a connection to old friends or a familiar place, a sense of ourselves that we'd grown good at, attached to, confident of. Those endings necessarily come before there's anything concrete to replace them with.

That space between the old and the new is limbo. Limbo can bring with it the feeling of emptiness: something has been lost, and there's nothing there yet to fill the void. Often limbo is so uncomfortable that we rush to fill it as quickly as possible. Particularly in a hurry-up society, we feel compelled to do or have something—anything—simply to avoid the feeling of doing or having nothing.

One way to use Repack is as a buffer against the demands of everyday life. Take the time to consider with care what you need and what you don't need before you Act.

What is it time to let go of?

In what ways have you outgrown the identity that you've been wearing from your past?

You can repack your self as you repack your stuff.

Who Do You Think You Are?

When people say they don't know what they want, in fact, they usually do know. They just don't want to let go of what they have or what they're doing or who they're being. Or they think that they really shouldn't want what they want. Or that it's not possible for them to get what they want.

After all, who do I think I am, anyway?

Identity is at the heart of repacking.

To set a path for the next phase of your life, you have to know where you came from. You have to know your own story. If you're like most people, you've been too busy living the story of your life to take the time to sit down and write it.

But when it comes to identity, having a coherent story will help you feel more at home in your past and less fearful about your future. The point is to see the movie of your life as a coherent storyline rather than a series of isolated frames. When you do that, you make more sense of what you need to carry with you for the next step in the journey, and what you can safely, comfortably, and confidently leave behind.

So who do you think you are? What's your story?

Write Your Own Book

Many people say they want to write a book. What they mean is, they want to tell their story, share the lessons they've learned, connect with their friends, leave a written record for their children. They want to reflect on their own journey and find meaning and purpose as they look back on the things they've done and the places they've been.

To other people the idea sounds like too much work or too much self-involvement.

Either way, as a journal exercise the idea is a useful one. Even if you have no ambition to write a book, thinking of your story as a book is a tool for repacking.

In your journal, start by creating the table of contents that will appear in the front of your "my story" book. What are the chapter titles you'd give your life story? Where would the story begin? How would you organize the episodes? If you were going to group the chapters into different phases of life, what would you call those phases? And how would you connect them?

Think about where you are now. What's the title of the chapter you're working on at the moment? And most important, looking forward, what title would you give the next chapter? The next phase of your life? Would you call it "the adventure phase"? The "leisure phase"? The "give back phase"? Giving it a name will help you carry your story forward.

As you write your own story, don't confuse who you are with what you've done. You are not your résumé. Your story is not the sum total of the titles you've held or the positions you've earned. Build on your story, but don't be limited by it. Use the lessons learned to create the next chapter, to extend your old story into a future of new possibilities.

There's an old saying that asks us, "If you are what you do, who are you when you don't?" Repacking is a reminder that to go after "What's next?" you can't still be living in "what's past."

Compared to Whom?

It's easy to lose track of yourself if you start comparing your story to other people's stories. Life Reimagined is based on the proposition that everyone's life is an experiment of one. So why waste time comparing your story to anyone else's? You can always find someone who's better than you—or worse, for that matter—in some way or another: richer, thinner, smarter, funnier.

The question is, what difference does it make?

Does comparing yourself to someone else help you discover your unique purpose?

Does measuring your life against someone else's give you helpful direction for moving forward?

The more you compare your story with anyone else's, the more you increase the chance that you'll derail your own journey.

The whole point of Life Reimagined is to be who you are and to start where you are.

Chapter 10

Act—What To Do Now?

In the end—actually, for there to be a beginning—you have to act. It all starts when you do *something*.

It's that basic: to reimagine your life, you have to do something. And then you do it again. Or you do something else based on the feedback you got from what you did. Or how it felt to you when you did it.

Start where you are. Use the preparation you've done and the practices you've worked on as guidance, input, creative juice. And then take a first step in a new direction. After that, adapt as you go.

It's really that simple. Take action.

The only thing worse than doing something that might be wrong is doing nothing at all—which can't be right.

Action Is the Enemy of Fear

Let's get this issue out of the way right away.

Here are some voices we all have in our heads:

What if I make a mistake?

What if I look foolish?

What if I do the wrong thing, and it doesn't work out the way I want it to?

What if my friends criticize me?

What if my family doesn't approve?

Here's the truth: Fear is the enemy of action. Fear robs you of your choices, saps your curiosity, short-circuits your courage.

But here's an even more powerful truth: action is the enemy of fear. Action disrupts fear and creates new possibilities and new energy. There is nothing more exhilarating than doing something new and learning from it.

Another truth: Life Reimagined is not a pass-fail test.

There's no need to make this process difficult, complicated, or anxiety producing. Despite what others might tell you, this is not "the first day of the rest of your life." You are not making some irrevocable commitment to a course of action that binds you to a path of no return. You are simply using choice, curiosity, and courage to take a first step toward a reimagined life that offers you a new sense of purpose.

As for those voices of fear and criticism—hit the mute button!

There are no grades, no teachers, no authority figures handing out judgments about how well or how poorly you're doing.

After all, how do you grade an adventure?

How do you evaluate the experiment-of-one that is your life?

All you need is your own permission to step out into the journey you've chosen and see how it feels to you.

The Status Quo Has No Status

Let's say you're stuck. Or you simply like the way things are right now.

Not acting will not keep the status quo in place. Things will change.

For that matter, it's important to remember that the status quo wasn't always the status quo: before it became the status quo, it was new, unfamiliar, untried, even uncomfortable. Acting not only opens up the path before you; acting also created the path behind you, the one that brought you here.

Nothing ever stays the way it is. Triggers will see to it that your life changes.

So the question is, who's in charge of your life?

Even attempting to embrace the status quo and to preserve it means turning over your life to forces outside yourself. It means turning away from choice and accepting whatever happens to you.

There's nothing wrong with feeling stuck.

There's nothing right with allowing yourself to stay stuck.

You Are the Expert on Your Own Life

Advice is useful. A Sounding Board will help. None of us should go it alone.

That said, trust your own gut. You are the expert on your own life. You are the only one who knows what works for you, what matters to you, what wants to happen through you.

After all the reflection and discussion, the evaluation and consideration, taking action is the only way to discover what is true for you. Taking action produces real knowledge, knowledge rooted in experience, not just thought.

If you have an idea, a dream, a hope, an aspiration, and you never act on it, you'll never know what could have been.

Until you try something, and it does or does not make sense in the context of your own experience, it's all just talk.

Serendipity Happens

Think of this as the Life Reimagined bumper sticker: Serendipity happens!

What that means is that taking action opens up all kinds of possibilities. Once you start to act, you allow surprises to happen. New connections can occur. Chance encounters can change the course you thought—you expected—you would be on. A planned meeting can lead to an unexpected introduction—someone knows someone who knows someone—and suddenly an opportunity you never expected and never even saw coming presents itself for your consideration.

Serendipity is a signal that you're on your way to your next chapter. It is a reward you get for taking action—for being willing to open yourself up to whatever happens, in whatever way it happens. It reminds you that there is no one right answer for your life. Rather, there are many real possibilities waiting for you to discover them—or for them to discover you.

Serendipity can open big doors.

Sometimes you think you know what to expect on the other side—and it isn't there.

Sometimes you have no idea what to expect—and life rewards you.

Regardless of what happens as you go through a new door, the important thing is that as you open the door, you are opening yourself up to Life Reimagined. You're embracing a life skill and practicing a mindset that will help define and create the rest of your life. You are learning to see and act in a powerful, creative way.

Sometimes things just work—usually because you're working at something.

Life As Improv

If you knew in advance how every minute of every day of the rest of your life would play out, would you feel better—or worse?

On the one hand, imagine the feeling of control it would give you. You would know with certainty exactly what to expect.

On the other hand, what a letdown! Where would the joy and surprise come from? Where would you find the chance to take risks or try experiments? You'd be accepting Life Unimagined for the rest of your life!

At its best, Life Reimagined is improvisational theater. A situation comes up, and you respond! Another actor throws you a line, and you make something up!

Living in the moment creates energy.

Experimenting on a daily basis is the way you take hold of a new outlook, a new attitude, possibly a new self-image.

It's how you change your "act"—literally. You think different, feel different, dress different, talk different.

And since it's *your* improvisation, if you don't like it, or you don't feel like it's working the way you want it to, you can change it!

Comic Serendipity

Sometimes the best way to act is to have an act.

That's what Gid Pool discovered.

"I'm one of these guys that gets bored real easy," he says of himself.

Which probably accounts for a résumé that includes a stint in the seminary and time in both the Army and the Air Force; a run as a ski instructor; a shot at being a financial planner; and a sales career that included selling boats, cars, insurance, and real estate.

And then, when he wasn't looking for it, Life Reimagined found him. Think of it as comic serendipity.

"My wife was a school guidance counselor, and her principal took a class at a comedy club," Gid explains.

At the end of the class, there was a night when the students got up on stage. Gid accompanied his wife to the show to catch the principal's act.

"The principal was funny," recalls Gid, "and then at the end of the show there was an announcement that there was another class starting."

For Gid, what happened next wasn't a question of careful planning or balancing the pros and cons. It was about trying something, about doing something to see what would happen.

"I wanted to try it because it looked fun," he remembers. "So I thought, if I can just go through the class and do the class show and not embarrass myself, then it'll be worth it. So I signed up before I left."

That was a Life Reimagined moment for Gid.

Not knowing what to expect and without anything in the way of preparation, Gid found himself suddenly engaged with a new, unanticipated possibility.

"When I took that comedy class," he says, "wow! What if I could really do this! What if this was the one thing I could hook myself into and just see how far I can go!"

Looking back now, it's hard to say whether Gid hooked into the comedy or the comedy hooked into him. What started as a class has become a passion and a calling.

"I've had jobs where I won't say I mailed it in," he says, comparing his newfound act to his old ones, "but I didn't sit up at night worrying about how well I was doing my job. Now I stay up to one or two in the morning looking at videos of me on stage. Changing things, adding things to make it better."

As a professional comic, Gid takes his humor very seriously. So much so, he's become a student of comedy.

For example, he can tell you the math formula it takes to qualify as a headliner.

"You need 18 seconds of laughs for every minute you're on stage," he says. "It's not just about being funny. It's about being funny enough."

Every successful comic has an act, and Gid is no exception. "I'm sort of like the 67-year-old guy who's looking out and saying, 'Here's what's wrong with the world. And I know how to fix it.'"

But behind the act is a man who is looking with appreciation at the new turn his reimagined life has given him. "It's a do-over," he says. "A chance to do something big and special with my life."

And what he's learned through a combination of action and serendipity he says applies to others as well.

"It happens almost every show," Gid says. "Someone will walk up to me and say, 'I always wanted to try that.' I say, 'Why don't you?' We're the first generation that gets a do-over. Why would we want to waste that on sitting around hoping we could try something instead of going out and doing it?"

Or, in the words of show business: Lights, camera, and, most important, action!

The Rhythm to Action

Getting started means taking action. Nothing happens until you take that first, courageous step.

But it doesn't mean taking heedless action. It doesn't mean putting your head down and pursuing a course without ever stopping, pausing, or looking up. Headlong and heedless action is as dangerous as no action at all. You end up far down a path without giving yourself the benefit of a midcourse correction.

There is, in fact, a rhythm to action. You act and then you reflect. First you go out into the world, and then you go back inside to see how your action feels. By moving back and forth between action and reflection, you take advantage of your experience; you learn from doing; and you capture the benefits of trying something new without feeling overcommitted to something that is still an improvisational experiment.

Take-a-Risk-a-Day Program

So how do you get started?

Here's an exercise to kick-start action, to start the process of action followed by reflection.

One small risk a day doesn't seem like too much to ask of yourself. Start with something easy. Start with where you are. Start with something you usually do—or don't do—because it's too ordinary.

Is there a shop or store close to your home, perhaps a boutique you've walked by a thousand times, but never gone into? Today go in.

Is there a server at a favorite lunch spot who has waited on you over and over, and you've never asked the person's name? Today introduce yourself and ask his or her name.

Is there a concert coming up near you, a performer you'd never ordinarily go to? Buy tickets. An Audubon Society walking path you've never gone on? Take a hike. A class at a community college that looks interesting? Enroll.

Sign up for your own take-a-risk-a-day program. For the next five days, take one risk each day—and then write about it in your journal.

Try stepping out of the no-risk zone into the possibility zone of Life Reimagined. At first it may feel a little scary. Or exhilarating. Or both.

But what you'll soon discover is that there are opportunities waiting for you, opportunities you didn't even know were possible.

You may confirm a talent, ignite a passion, or reconnect with a value you didn't remember you had.

As you go from action to reflection and back again, you'll find that the practice of Life Reimagined opens up real possibilities that connect you with a profound purpose that adds meaning to your life.

Chapter 11

Take a Break—Is It Over Yet?

You've gone through each of the six practices that make up the Life Reimagined map. So this must be the journey's end! Right?

Actually no.

In fact, the journey is never over. Remember Yogi Berra's famous dictum, "It ain't over 'til it's over"?

When it comes to the Life Reimagined journey, good old Yogi had it wrong. The truth is, it's never over.

When you reach Act, the sixth guidepost on the map, you haven't arrived at your destination. You've actually just started. Because after you Act, your next step is to Reflect. You pause and see how your action feels to you: Does it sit well? Is it uncomfortable in an uncomfortable way? Or is it uncomfortable in a satisfying way, like the first day at a gym doing a new exercise regime? You know that workout might make your muscles sore—and you also know you'll feel a little proud of yourself for having made the effort.

After you've gone around the Life Reimagined map for the first time, you'll want to check in with the members of your Sounding Board. You'll want to report in on how your journey is going. You'll want to invite their feedback, to add their insights to your own experiences.

You'll want to read through your journal. See what you've written at different steps in your journey. You'll want to take the time to add new entries that reflect on what you've learned, what confirmed your initial feelings, and what unexpected surprises have come your way.

Getting through the six practices doesn't mean that you stop your journey. Far from it: now you'll go back through each of the guideposts along the Life Reimagined map, until you return again to Act—and then you'll make the circuit again.

As you go around the Life Reimagined map, you'll gain new strengths, new awarenesses, a greater sense of your own capabilities, a fresh appreciation for your own gifts, passions, and values.

You'll get better and better at sensing what's authentic for you, at assessing what feels right and what doesn't feel right.

You'll appreciate even more the value of your Possibilities Journal.

You may find yourself visiting the Life Reimagined web site with more regularity. You may enroll in a new course, volunteer in a new program, travel someplace new. You may make a concerted effort to contact old friends—or to add new friends. You may discover that you are actually the entrepreneur of your own life—and that being an entrepreneur doesn't require you to open up a business. It simply requires you to open up your life.

As you go around the Life Reimagined circuit, you'll discover two other absolutely vital things.

First, you'll find that the more you practice Life Reimagined, the more you develop the essential life skills that we need for the 21st century—and that we need to make the most of the new phase of life.

Second, as you internalize the lessons and capabilities that Life Reimagined has to offer, you'll discover that Life Reimagined is a mindset. It's a new way of thinking and acting to meet the demands and opportunities of a new reality.

Adopting that mindset, making it *your* mindset, is the real promise of Life Reimagined.

Chapter 12

Is This Your Life Reimagined Moment?

Something is happening, and it affects us all. Life Reimagined—the new phase of life—is changing the entire life course.

At first you might not notice the subtle but powerful changes that are under way. But once you start looking for it, listening for it—simply noticing it—you'll discover that Life Reimagined is on everyone's mind.

It's everywhere around you. It's covered in newspaper reports and written up in magazine stories that shape conversations. It's embedded in political discussions of how we're living and where we're going. It's what we talk about over the dinner table and in emails and phone calls with family and friends. It's what comes up in sermons and commencement talks. It's the topic of discussions that range from everyday friends sharing their experiences in coffee shops to leaders trying to make sense of the way the world is changing.

Because it's everyone's story.

It's the shape of life today, the contour of the new territory. It is the defining spirit of our age, a movement. We are learning about it at the same time that we create it. It is everyone's moment.

They're Writing About Me!

There are pioneers and innovators everywhere who are taking a chance, exploring new possibilities, finding new directions.

Jump into a cab at a New York airport for the drive into the city and the cab driver has a story: he's turning forty years old, he's going through a divorce, and he's just made the decision to go back to flight school to get his recreational pilot's license. That's a Life Reimagined moment.

Sit down for a casual dinner at your favorite neighborhood restaurant and ask the woman who's serving you what's happening in her life. She has a story: she is in her early fifties and has just lost her job in a corporate downsizing. But she's not going to be a server for long. She's doing this job to learn about the restaurant business so she can start her own place. That's a Life Reimagined moment.

A friend in her forties tells you her story over coffee: she has reached a transition point in her career. But it's not about money; it's about what she does next. After a successful twenty-year run in a job that she's loved, she's feeling pulled to take on something new, far away, the adventure of her life. She's having a hard time making up her mind whether to go or to stay, and she wants to explore her options. That's a Life Reimagined moment.

Take a call from your older brother, who lives half a continent away. He wants to catch you up on his story: at age sixty-five, he retired from his position as a college professor. Now he and his wife have built their dream cottage on a lake in a small town, and he's going back to get serious about his favorite hobby—photography—because he loves taking pictures of nature. Doing anything more or anything different is on hold; photography is his passion, and he feels fulfilled. That's a Life Reimagined moment.

A friend who's about to turn fifty describes with great pride her eighty-one–year-old father. He's a retired physician in Boston who made the decision almost twenty years ago to learn Spanish. But not just conversational Spanish. He wanted to read the great Spanish literary classics in the original language and then be able to discuss them—in Spanish. He found a teacher in the Boston area and now, twenty years later, he's reading *Don Quixote* and *El Cid* in Spanish, writing his own essays in Spanish, and sending them to his teacher so they can discuss them—in Spanish. The kicker: his teacher has moved to Portugal, so they talk over Skype. The other kicker: based on her father's example, the friend's forty-nine–year-old sister has decided to take up the cello as her new pursuit so she can play the Bach Cello Suite in G Major, hopefully before she reaches eighty-one. Father and daughter are both having Life Reimagined moments.

If you read this book and you thought, "They're writing about me!"—you're right.

Life Reimagined is about you. It's about you, your family, your friends, and the people you've met in this book. Because it's about all of us.

Purpose and Connection

We can learn something about our lives today by talking with people who have traveled the path before us and asking them to look back in their own lives to where we are now.

When you ask them to assess their lives, they almost always mention one shared regret: they wish they had taken more chances to be true to themselves—to be more authentic.

In retrospect, they say, *they* were the biggest obstacle in their lives. They wish they had chosen to live with more curiosity and courage. They wish they had trusted themselves to be themselves.

No matter what their age, they realize that what they owned in life were their choices.

If that is the abiding regret, what is the underlying truth about choosing an authentic life? What is the core?

Both research and common sense agree: it all comes down to having a purpose and being connected to others.

Each of us has to discover our own purpose, our own reason for getting up in the morning. We have to make a journey inside before we can take ourselves out into the world. But this is not a journey into narcissism. Becoming clear and strong and confident about who you are really only matters if it makes it possible for you to connect with others, share with others, be of service to others.

Finding purpose and connecting with others is the core that generates an authentic life. We need to find ways in which we can stay engaged with life—by finding our purpose—and engaging in life—and by connecting with others.

Personal Manifesto

The world turns on stories. We each have our own story. Our stories reflect our purpose and our connections.

Personal manifestos are woven into the stories in this

book, the stories in your life, the stories we share, regardless of age or time or place.

We can choose.

Choosing is central to our well-being, to our freedom, to our authenticity. Choosing is our expression of personal purpose. Choosing is how we tell ourselves and others what matters. Our choices matter—and ultimately, mattering matters.

We can stay curious.

The way we learn, change, and ultimately connect is through curiosity. Curiosity keeps us open to new experiences and new people. No matter what our age, we have more to discover about ourselves, more to learn about others, and more to explore.

We can act courageously.

It takes courage to be who you are. It takes courage to take yourself into the world. It takes courage to respond positively to the triggers of life. Living courageously means we own our own time, our own choices, our own curiosity. It means we live with purpose and connection, finding our way to the most fulfilling lives we can create.

What Is the Life Reimagined Mindset?

Life Reimagined is a new mindset that is creating a powerful movement that matches the emerging moment that we are in.

Life Reimagined is a call to live our lives with purpose and connection as we answer the "What's next?" question.

It is a mindset—a way you experience the world. It is a way to see the world differently. Looked at through the lens of Life Reimagined, the world appears different when you wake up in the morning. You see possibilities instead of problems. Your eyes, your brain, your heart are focused on a different vista. You've adopted a purpose point of view.

The Difference a Mindset Makes

The changes that mark the Life Reimagined movement are as simple and powerful as a set of transformations, shifts from the old story to the new story.

We are shifting from an old story that was about aging to a new story that is about living.

From an old story that was about retiring to a new story that is about reimagining.

From an old story that was about growing old to a new story that is about growing whole.

From an old story that was about declining to a new story that is about discovering.

From an old story that was about having answers to a new story that is about living in questions.

From an old story that was about getting advice to a new story that is about getting allies.

And from an old story that was about contracting to a new story that is about connecting.

A Life Reimagined mindset becomes a lens for making sense of the new story that touches our lives. It gives us a way to see everyday life so a pattern begins to emerge—a pattern that suggests the path to real possibilities.

But the lens is not rose-colored. There is nothing unrealistically romantic or make-believe about the Life Reimagined mindset.

Make no mistake: the triggers of life will inevitably knock you off balance, off course, off center.

When that happens—and it will happen, over and over—Life Reimagined helps reframe the experience. The manifesto, map, and practices of Life Reimagined will give you a way to regain your balance more quickly, to find the way forward with more confidence, to adapt to new circumstances with more courage, and to make the choices that guide you in life with more purpose.

Knowing full well that there is no predictable future, much less a perfect one, you still have the opportunity and the responsibility to imagine what your future can be. Regardless of how old you are now, regardless of how old you will live to be, the essential questions remain the same: Where do you want to go next? With whom? Doing what? Living where? For what purpose?

The good news and the bad news of growing up and growing older are the same: you have no one else to blame if you do not live a life of your own imagining. You are in charge of your own experiment of one.

What Is the Movement?

The question at the center of the Life Reimagined movement is "What's next?"

That's where we end this book.

What happens next?

What happens next in your life?

Will you embrace Life Reimagined as a mindset? Will you join the Life Reimagined movement? Will you seize the moment and use the map and guideposts of Life Reimagined to learn the life skills required for the new phase of life?

And what will happen next for all of us?

Life Reimagined is a movement that is asking us to join.

It is a rallying cry that touches us regardless of age.

It is a movement that crosses the boundaries of age and income, race and gender. It is a movement that speaks to each of us and to all of us.

It talks about living your life on purpose. It talks about connecting all our lives in common purpose.

What Is the Moment?

This is a movement that reflects the moment we're in—and the real possibilities we believe in.

It's your moment. A moment of the new emerging life phase that is one of the most powerful social movements of our time. It's a moment where we shed old myths and dismiss old preconceptions of how we live our lives. In this moment, we can sense a conversation that is waiting to happen, responsibilities waiting to be addressed, real possibilities waiting to be seized.

It's up to you—and to all of us—to choose with curiosity and courage the life you want to create for yourself and the future we all want to share.

Pioneer of Life Reimagined: Jane Pauley

Jane Pauley is one of the authentic ambassadors of the Life Reimagined movement. A four-time Emmy Award winner, Jane is an American icon as a television anchor and journalist. For 13 years she was the co-host of NBC's *The Today Show,* after which she had a 12-year stint as co-host of *Dateline NBC.* Jane is the author of an autobiography, *Skywriting: A Life Out of the Blue.*

Since her 2001 diagnosis of bipolar disorder, Jane has been an outspoken advocate for integrative medicine and all aspects of wellness. Currently she hosts a segment on *The Today Show* called "Life Reimagined," which features stories of ordinary people using Life Reimagined to discover extraordinary possibilities in their lives.

Q: Life Reimagined is about helping people discover what's next in their lives. Have you always had an idea of what you were meant to do?

Jane Pauley: Some people are blessed with a very clear sense of what interests them early in life. For me it wasn't that way. What a relief to get to this point in my life, where I kind of understand how it all linked up! The reason that's nice is not just because it feels better when you feel solid and not fuzzy at the edges, but it helped point me toward a future direction. Not that I know where I'm headed! But it's kind of validating.

Q: You had a Life Reimagined moment in your career that caused a great deal of comment in the world of television: when you let it be known that you didn't really want to do *The Today Show* any more. What happened?

Jane Pauley: I was sitting in a lecture hall at the first parents' weekend at my son's college. He was a freshman. And I went to a lecture and the professor was talking about work. And what is good work. He wrote on the board in big words: number one, the key aspect of good work is alignment. Being in alignment with the work of the organization, the mission, or what you're doing.

Number two was being regularly, if not constantly, reinforced in that alignment.

And as happy as I should have been, as lucky as I was, as blessed as I was in my career, I knew I was not in alignment. And in that moment, in that chair, and at that parents' weekend, I knew it was time for me to leave a primetime television show.

Q: One of the key ideas of Life Reimagined is that none of us should go it alone and that isolation is fatal. What are your thoughts about that?

Jane Pauley: It's really important that we expose ourselves to other people who might one day randomly say something about you. Because we're not paying attention to who we are. We look in the mirror, but it takes other people seeing us and knowing us to identify what makes us special.

I really think it's necessary to be a molecule out there amongst other molecules. That's how you have those opportunities to randomly have those insights that allow you to go forward. Actively getting something going. Even if it's not the right exact something, acting is more important than sitting in the chair like "The Thinker" waiting for what your perfect insight is going to be. It's counterintuitive, but it works better if you just get out there and start doing something.

There's a phrase in business: "If you don't know where you're going, any road will get you there." I take that to mean if you don't know where you're going, just go! Pick a road and go! You'll find something. Something that works, something that doesn't. Just get something going. But not at high speed. You don't need to rush into this road. You can walk. You can walk the road.

Q: There's a sense that Life Reimagined matches the moment that we're in and that it's poised to become a movement. What do you think is the idea that's in the air right now?

Jane Pauley: The idea that we're all in it together. As baby boomers, we have always all been in it together! We've never had an original gesture, an original idea! Because there were so many of us that, if even a fraction of us decided to wear bangs, suddenly a million people are wearing bangs!

I think the biggest thing is merely the idea that the baby boomers got wind of their future possibilities. And we're all in it together and always have been.

Chapter 13

It's Your Move

Let's end this book where we started.

In the end it's up to you.

Will you choose to take your Life Reimagined journey?

Will you choose to add your story to the thousands—the millions—of stories of curious, courageous pioneers of Life Reimagined?

Will you choose to join the Life Reimagined movement?

Here's why it matters—why what we all do matters.

We're at the beginning of something powerful and important: the Life Reimagined movement.

It's a movement that is personal in its touch and widespread in its reach.

It's a movement that is reimagining more than 50 years of accepted practice and conventional wisdom about the trajectory and purpose of our lives.

This movement does away with outdated boundaries, ir-relevant conventions, and unproductive expectations. It challenges a system that has emerged to tell us how society expects us to live our lives.

Because of this movement we are shifting from an old story of a single, predictable trajectory prescribed by social convention to a new story of Life Reimagined and a new way of living that enables each of us to decide our own path, our own journey.

The old story drew the path of life as a simple parabola—you went up one side, down the other. Life Reimagined says there's a new life curve, where choice, curiosity, and courage offer each of us the real possibility of discovery and learning throughout an increasingly long life.

In a world that's changing it's time for us to change—to take on our deepest fears and take hold of our greatest aspirations.

It's your movement.

It's your move.

A New Way of Living

We are learning to think differently about the possibilities for our lives and to act differently to make those possibilities real.

Whether pushed by pain or pulled by possibilities, we are entering a new era in which our own choices create a new real-ity. We know that it's never too late—or too soon—to discover new paths for our lives. We know that we can choose a new way of living at any age to embrace our own purpose and our connections to others.

The way things used to be is not the way they are now—

and certainly not the way they will be as we go forward. We are moving rapidly, powerfully, and inexorably into a new territory that opens new possibilities.

We can all feel it: things are changing quickly. And the changes, as they come, will be deep, powerful, and permanent.

The Handbook of the Life Reimagined Movement

This book is the handbook of the Life Reimagined movement. The ideas and practices in these pages and on the Life Reimagined web site will equip you to make sense of the changes going on in the world. And they'll equip you to make choices for your own life—your own way of living—moving ahead. The stories of the Life Reimagined innovators and pioneers will give you confidence, the sure knowledge that you are not alone on this journey. They show that your Life Reimagined moment is defined not so much what you do but as the way in which you do it.

In this book we introduced you to a new way of living, a mindset embodied by five essential truths of Life Reimagined:

1. We need to live our lives with choice, curiosity, and courage at all ages.

2. In a world of change there are two constants: having your own purpose and being connected to others.

3. We are each an experiment of one. There is no one-size-fits-all answer for the new phase of life.

4. Life Reimagined is a journey of inner and outer discovery. The ultimate discovery each of us can make is self-discovery.

5.   Don't go it alone. Isolation is fatal.

We are at the beginning of the Life Reimagined move-ment. Moving forward, there is much work to be done by each of us, for all of us.

Here is what we set out to do in this book—and what we need to do together:

- Debunk the old policies and outmoded practices that stand in the way of our new way of living. And we need to create the new policies and practices that will advance it. *Our task is to challenge the past and at the same time to reimagine the future.*

- Find the right language to express this emerging movement, a vocabulary that gives shape to the new realities and gives voice to our aspirations. *Changing the way we think and act in our lives means changing the way we talk about our new possibilities.*

- Collect and amplify the stories of the pioneers of this movement. Stories are how we share experiences and how we learn from one another. This book and the Life Reimagined web site capture the life lessons of some of the early explorers. But Life Reimagined exists in thousands—millions—of variations. *We need a living library of each of these stories—including yours.*

- Express accurately and clearly the mindset of the Life Reimagined movement. Life Reimagined has a powerful manifesto, a strong and vital point of view. *Articulating that mindset, stating that manifesto, is how we build the movement.*

- Build the community of Life Reimagined. The Life Reimagined movement is both intensely personal and powerfully universal. If you read this book and find something to try in your own life, something to share with your family and your friends, something to talk about or something to explore, something to build on or something to disagree with, then the Life Reimagined movement is growing. *Ultimately, for the movement to succeed, Life Reimagined needs to touch our lives in real ways—and connect us to other people's lives in new ways.*

Stay Connected

Throughout this book and on the Life Reimagined web site you will find opportunities to stay engaged and connected. We hope you take advantage of those opportunities. When you connect with us and with each other—when you share your thoughts and insights, your stories and your experiences—the community grows and the Life Reimagined movement spreads.

You embark on your own Life Reimagined journey.

In the end it's up to you.

In the end it starts with you.

In the end it's your move.

Life Reimagined Conversations

Life Reimagined takes on a whole new dimension when you use the book as the basis for conversations—with partners, friends, family, colleagues.

But before you get a group together for a Life Reimagined conversation, take the following steps:

1. Read this book.

2. Begin your Possibilities Journal.

3. Highlight the book and make notes; list your own questions in your journal.

Getting a group together to talk about Life Reimagined is a good way to generate even more energy around the Life Reimagined journey, both for yourself and others. In a variety of ways we feed off one another's ideas, stories and insights. The result benefits everyone.

Here are 10 questions to help you start conversations at

home, at work, in your book group, at your place of worship, or in your social circle.

1. Do you agree that there is a new phase of life between middle age and old age, with unique characteristics and possibilities? If yes, what are some examples of Life Reimagined that you know of?

2. Is reimagining really necessary? When is it not necessary?

3. Before reading this book, did you think about a longer life as a problem or a possibility—or both? Did the book change your mind?

4. The stories throughout the book portray people who make choices to live more fulfilling lives. Would you consider doing the same? What choices are you considering?

5. Do you consider working longer in the new phase of life a burden or an opportunity? Is there something you've always wanted to do but haven't yet done?

6. Do you feel the desire to get up in the morning committed to making a difference? Do you feel it more strongly now?

7. What are several of your journal entries that you consider contain your most powerful insights?

8. Were you inspired by anyone in the book—or any ideas in the book—to make a change in your thinking or in your life? By whom or by what?

9. Are there particular Life Reimagined messages or practices that you think would apply to people of all ages? What are they?

10. Other: What question would *you* like to discuss?

Acknowledgments

As we observed remarkable people all over the country who are reimagining their lives, we were struck over and over again by the truth that no one does anything that truly matters alone. This book is no exception. We're grateful for all the people who made this journey possible for us. They have all been great partners, and many have become good friends.

We want to extend our deep thanks and appreciation to AARP's CEO A. Barry Rand. From the beginning and at every step of the way, Barry has given his unconditional support to Life Reimagined. This book owes much to his vision and generous spirit. Emilio Pardo and Rick Bowers, two of AARP's greatest talents, contributed their boundless energy, far-ranging ideas, and purposeful leadership to this project. Their mark can be found in the best part of this book. And they are more than contributors—they are friends of the heart, fearless trailblazers, enduring traveling companions, and leaders of the Life Reimagined movement.

Keith Yamashita and his colleagues at SYPartners have given selflessly to the Life Reimagined undertaking. Keith provided invaluable coaching and wise advice. We owe a huge debt of gratitude to Susan Schuman, Nicholas Anderson, Nicolas Maitret, Jessica Orkin, Kacie Wise, Emily Goldstein, Rachel Berger, and the others on the SYP team for all the ways in which they shaped and shepherded Life Reimagined through the creative process.

Our thanks go as well to David DeCheser and the team at R/GA. Their remarkable blend of imagination and technology is responsible for bringing Life Reimagined to life online.

We have benefitted in ways large and small from the experience, wisdom, and insights of Life Reimagined thought leaders and scouts. Our thanks go to Stuart Brown, Kate Ebner, Rich Feller, Steve Gillon, Christopher Metzler, Stephan Rechtshaffen, Linda Spradley Dunn, Janet Taylor, Bill Thomas, and John Hendricks for helping to bring the Life Reimagined point of view to life.

No project of the magnitude of Life Reimagined happens without the support of backers, sponsors, champions, and co-conspirators; our own group is as wide as it is exceptional. Our thanks go to Gail Aldrich, JoAnn Jenkins, Barbara Shipley, Jodi Lipson, Beth Domingo, Fritz Yuvancic, Dara Padwo-Audick, Kim Sedmak, C. B. Wismar, Wade Osborne, Anne Herbster, Terry Pittman, and Cyrus Bamji.

From the beginning we have had the wise insight and steady guidance of Steve Piersanti at Berrett-Koehler Publishers; his flawless orchestration helped bring this book to fruition. To David Marshall go our thanks for his unerring advice in navigating the digital landscape, along with Richard Wilson,

Acknowledgments

Dianne Platner, Michael Crowley, Jeevan Sivasubramaniam, Kristen Frantz, Katie Sheehan, and the rest of the BK team.

Life Reimagined contains the accounts of a number of people whose stories illustrate the down-to-earth ways we each can reimagine our lives. Many thanks to Betty Smith, Rich Luker, Barb Timberlake, Paulie Gee, Gid Pool, Tripp Hanson, Maria Vasquez, Annie Walker, and John Drury for sharing their stories.

And there are some others on the national scene, true Life Reimagined pioneers, who have been willing both to tell their stories and to make Life Reimagined part of the larger conversation. Many thanks to Jane Pauley, Emilio Estefan, James "J. B." Brown, and Chris Gardner.

And finally, to Sally Leider and Frances Diemoz, our partners in love and in life, we extend our deep gratitude for enduring our absences and encouraging our pursuits. For us, they embody the truths that are in this book and are living proof of what it means to reimagine your life—and why it matters. Without them, there would be no book.

Richard J. Leider
Minneapolis, Minnesota

Alan M. Webber
Santa Fe, New Mexico

Richard J. Leider

Q: How do you describe yourself?

Richard Leider: I love the line by T. S. Eliot: "Old men ought to be explorers." I'm an explorer. What does that mean? It means that I'm personally burying the old story of retirement. I'm enlarging the real possibilities of my life right now, not retiring from them.

Q: Interesting. What's next for you?

Richard Leider: One of my colleagues calls me "the Pope of Purpose." A bit of a stretch, for sure. But for more than four decades, I've dedicated myself to helping people find their purpose—their reason for getting up in the morning. My curiosity about this has taken me as a keynote speaker to all 50 states, Canada, and four continents. Along the way, I've written eight books (now nine!), including two international bestsellers, *Repacking Your Bags* and *The Power of Purpose*. Also, I've fit in time to lead 28 walking safaris in Tanzania. I "bagged" 30 sleeping-bag nights last year. My goal is 40 nights a year sleeping out—in a tent. I feel that I'm in my prime time in both my life and my work. For me, it's time to move forward, not to look backward, and change the conversation for the better and forever.

Q: What's it like to work with Alan?

Richard Leider: We both like adventure. All kinds. To me working together felt like an intellectual adventure. A journey of curiosity. Alan's one of the toughest critics I ever met. And, at the same time, one of the most curious and compassionate people I've ever met. He cares a great deal. As a result his insights mean the most to me. Nobody intrigues me more than Alan. Rarely does a conversation between us go by that I'm not making mental notes or spending valuable time later contemplating his words. It's quite a gift to work together. And it's fun. Alan is playful and incredibly funny.

Q: What was your writing process?

Richard Leider: It's hard to explain simply the alchemy of synergy. It's a mystery. With two of us writing it was like mixing up a good dish. First, you start with separate ingredients—ideas.

Then you take what's there and mix it up. Often, not always, you emerge with something so much better, so much more palatable, that you cannot imagine that anything different was ever intended in the first place. We need curiosity to live. It's as essential as bread to eat. Conspiring, creating, and now, writing with Alan has become an essential part of my diet.

Q: Anything else about yourself and Life Reimagined?

Richard Leider: We set out to capture the "voice" of the Life Reimagined movement. That was our creative challenge. We wanted to be of service, to be human, to connect at the core with ordinary folks. We wanted to create a work that would change the conversation from aging to living. People would want to pass it on to their spouse, partner, or best friends. We said at the end of the Introduction, "Things are about to get interesting." That's true for Alan and me. We're eager ourselves to continue the conversation and, maybe, the writing.

Oh, one last thing. One of the benefits of writing a book is that you get to give a public proclamation of gratitude to people. So, Alan, thanks! It definitely looks interesting.

Alan M. Webber

Judy Tuwaletstiwa

Q: How do you describe yourself?

Alan Webber: At the moment I've given myself the title "Global Detective." It's a way of describing a fully engaged life that involves speaking, traveling, writing, and trying to make sense out of all the change going on in the world. And trying, at the same time, to contribute to making the world change for the better.

Q: Cute. What else have you done in your life?

Alan Webber: Hey, no need to get snide! In more conventional terms, I've worked as a journalist—as managing editor and editorial director of the *Harvard Business Review* and co-founder of *Fast Company* magazine; in government and politics at the local, state, and federal level; I've been a fellow of both German and Japanese foundations; served on the boards of a number of nonprofit organizations; and written books, articles, and columns.

Q: Aren't you being a little modest? Who are some of the people you've interviewed or worked with in your career?

Alan Webber: Between HBR, *Fast Company,* and my new career as a Global Detective, I've had a chance to interview and work with remarkable people all over the world: the Dalai Lama, Muhammad Yunus, Paulo Coelho, Brother David Steindl-Rast, Isabel Allende, Frank Gehry—the list goes on and on. A lot of what I learned from those people and others, such as Jim Collins, Tom Peters, Seth Godin, Dan Pink, who are more in the world of business and entrepreneurship, is in my book, *Rules of Thumb: 52 Truths for Winning at Business Without Losing Your Self.* Oh, one more thing: I once spent a summer catching fly balls during batting practice with the St. Louis Cardinals—a personal best!

Q: What is your personal stake in Life Reimagined?

Alan Webber: To paraphrase the old advertisement on TV, "I'm not just an author about Life Reimagined, I'm also a participant in it!" I left *Fast Company* magazine in 2003 after 10 of the most intense years of my life, working as an entrepreneur and an editor, bringing a dream to life and watching it flourish. Then I moved to Santa Fe with my wife—and all of a sudden I was challenged to reimagine my life! So when it comes to writing about Life Reimagined and embracing real possibilities, I can honestly say that I not only have written about it, I'm also living it.

Q: What's it like to write a book with Richard Leider?

Alan Webber: Amazing. Fantastic. Educational. Inspiring. Richard is a perfect colleague and mentor—wise in so many ways, fun to work with, easy to work with, generous and encouraging. But more than that, he is unbelievably knowledgeable about people on a granular level. How people grow and learn, how they shy away from tough decisions, how they can be encouraged to try new things. And most important, how people go about finding real purpose in their lives.

Q: So how do two people write a book together?

Alan Webber: We very quickly developed a simple working process. We sketched out the ideas in the book and the outline, chapter by chapter. We'd get together and Richard would have outlined his thoughts about the points we needed to make in each chapter; then we'd blend our thoughts. I'd listen to Richard talk through his points and take careful notes. I'd write a page or half a page to feed back what Richard had said. Then came the good part: we'd read it out loud and we'd discuss whether or not, between the two of us, we had gotten it right. After that it was shampoo, rinse, repeat! Richard and I have read every word of this book out loud to each other many times in the course of writing it. It's meant to sound like a conversation between two friends who genuinely care about the ideas and about each other—because that's the way it was written.

Q: Anything else about yourself and Life Reimagined?

Alan Webber: To me, this book is fundamentally true. The things it says apply to me, in my own life. I know that, as we wrote it, I found myself measuring my own thoughts and actions against what we were writing for others. And I easily found places where I fell short in meeting our own prescription! And also was encouraged to be more courageous! I also know that there are truths in this book for my two children, Adam and Amanda, who are both in their 30s. Life Reimagined crosses the old borders and boundaries of age and generation, income and status, geography, and gender. As we say in the book, it is both personal and universal.

What's Next?

Dear readers,

This is a book that has no ending.

That's the whole point. So rather than have you read the book and close it, we've created exclusive "what's next" content—easy ways for you to continue your Life Reimagined journey. You'll find it all at www.LifeReimagined.org/next.

These stories, tools, and activities will help you find your passion, connect with your Sounding Board, and live the life you're meant to live.

- Explore local events that support your journey.

- Meet other readers in your community.

- Watch inspiring videos on the people you've read about in this book.

- View inspiring, engaging stories and share your own.

The Life Reimagined journey continues!

Richard J. Leider   Alan M. Webber

Index

Index

Index

Index

Berrett–Koehler
Publishers

Berrett-Koehler is an independent publisher dedicated to an ambitious mission: *Creating a World That Works for All*.

We believe that to truly create a better world, action is needed at all levels—individual, organizational, and societal. At the individual level, our publications help people align their lives with their values and with their aspirations for a better world. At the organizational level, our publications promote progressive leadership and management practices, socially responsible approaches to business, and humane and effective organizations. At the societal level, our publications advance social and economic justice, shared prosperity, sustainability, and new solutions to national and global issues.

A major theme of our publications is "Opening Up New Space." Berrett-Koehler titles challenge conventional thinking, introduce new ideas, and foster positive change. Their common quest is changing the underlying beliefs, mindsets, institutions, and structures that keep generating the same cycles of problems, no matter who our leaders are or what improvement programs we adopt.

We strive to practice what we preach—to operate our publishing company in line with the ideas in our books. At the core of our approach is stewardship, which we define as a deep sense of responsibility to administer the company for the benefit of all of our "stakeholder" groups: authors, customers, employees, investors, service providers, and the communities and environment around us.

We are grateful to the thousands of readers, authors, and other friends of the company who consider themselves to be part of the "BK Community." We hope that you, too, will join us in our mission.

A BK Life Book

This book is part of our BK Life series. BK Life books change people's lives. They help individuals improve their lives in ways that are beneficial for the families, organizations, communities, nations, and world in which they live and work. To find out more, visit **www.bk-life.com**.

Berrett–Koehler
Publishers

A community dedicated to creating
a world that works for all

Dear Reader,

Thank you for picking up this book and joining our worldwide community of Berrett-Koehler readers. We share ideas that bring positive change into people's lives, organizations, and society.

To welcome you, we'd like to offer you a free ebook. You can pick from among twelve of our bestselling books by entering the promotional code **BKP92E** here: http://www.bkconnection.com/welcome.

When you claim your free ebook, we'll also send you a copy of our e-newsletter, the *BK Communiqué*. Although you're free to unsubscribe, there are many benefits to sticking around. In every issue of our newsletter you'll find

- A free ebook
- Tips from famous authors
- Discounts on spotlight titles
- Hilarious insider publishing news
- A chance to win a prize for answering a riddle

Best of all, our readers tell us, "Your newsletter is the only one I actually read." So claim your gift today, and please stay in touch!

Sincerely,

Charlotte Ashlock
Steward of the BK Website

Questions? Comments? Contact me at bkcommunity@bkpub.com.